HARDWIRING VS. REWIRING

SHAPING THE MINDSET, SKILLSET, AND BEHAVIORS DURING EARLY CHILDHOOD DEVELOPMENT STAGES

Ravi Rajaratnam, Ph.D.

DEDICATION

I dedicate this book to my dearly departed brother, Mohan Rajaratnam, who left us suddenly on November 21, 2021.

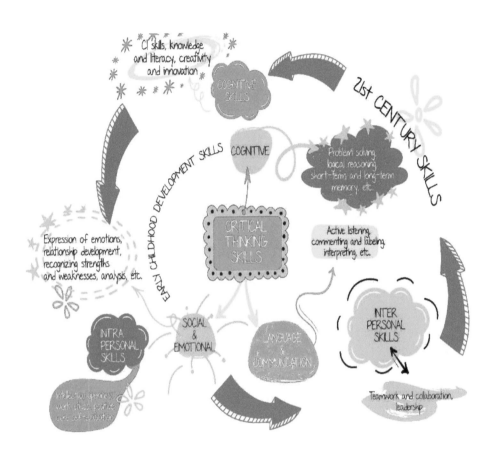

PROLOGUE

Why is there so much unrest around the world? Unrest and upheavals spanning societal, economic, and political realms and creating a polarized society. Why is our community suffering from a severe lack of attention and focus? Why have we not become the best version of ourselves? Why are we overly anxious, stressed, and more depressed than we have ever been before? The continuous negative trajectory of increased moral decay, unrest, and upheaval has taken an enormous toll and will continue to harm society and the environment. Can we do anything to turn this around and recover, or are we all doomed? These questions may have also come to your mind. But unfortunately, many of us "live with" these perceived or actual ills, disparity, pain, and injustice and continue with our day-to-day life, providing for our family, playing our respective roles, and contributing to society to the best of our capability. I, for one, was guilty of doing this as well until the day I told myself there had to be something more that I could do.

Sometimes, during our life journey, most of us ask ourselves, "What is my purpose, and how is this world a better place with my existence?" Whether by our contribution to our family, community, or the environment, most of us contribute positively to society.

Regularly, I try to take stock of how I make this world a better place. During one of these moments of reflection, I became determined to explore the root causes of these problems that I labeled "ills." I have always been an avid and passionate reader - specifically, non-fiction. I have listened to many podcasts and have always tried to look at multiple and opposing viewpoints before arriving at my balanced and educated judgments – right, wrong or indifferent. The decisions and conclusions are mainly influenced by my first-hand experience, having worked for three decades in the corporate world and reviewing multiple research articles.

I have examined the empirical findings from numerous research studies, together with other trusted sources (thought leaders), most of which are backed by scientific evidence, in an attempt to connect the dots. I specifically want to answer the question, "What makes human beings behave and operate the way we do daily? What causes our biases, either conscious or unconscious?" To answer the above questions, I've decided to explore the "shaping" mechanism that has influenced our lives since we came into this world. Is there a way that we can hardwire the desirable traits that help shape us to become exemplary citizens? I've dedicated the bulk of this book to discussing these traits; I will refer to them as "positive traits." At the same time, I acknowledge that what's considered "positive" to one individual might not be universal. However, I would encourage you to have an open mind and review the information to determine the impact of hardwiring on positive traits during the early childhood development stages. I would also encourage you to look at the facts presented in this book, substantiate these good traits as desirable, and stress that common sense still prevails.

My initial goal for this book was to serve as a reference guide for parents of young children, caregivers, and educators for a series of children's books that will help form these good traits. It was meant to be a manual on reinforcing the messages in the children's books so that the positive attributes can be hardwired at an early age as part of the child's early development skills journey.

However, going back to my decades-old practical experience in various leadership roles, I was quickly reminded that to be a good leader, you need to excel in self-leadership and awareness to effect change and to be an effective role model for others. Therefore, this book will go beyond the first intention to serve as a manual and further explain "the why" and "the how" so you can appreciate the science behind the recommended teaching and why you need to adopt them.

The information in this book will also benefit adults who are on their self-improvement journey and looking to excel in their lives, both personally and professionally. It does not matter the stage you're currently in life, nor if you are struggling to make sense of the large volume of resources available on how to rewire your mind. The knowledge provided in this book will help you jump-start and accelerate the rewiring process, especially when you are aware of the key "connective tissue," which will be explained later.

In my quest for the root cause of behavior and actions that contribute to societal, economic, and political ills, it became evident that there is a strong correlation between early childhood development skills and 21st-century skills; precisely, skills that are critical in our current digital industrial revolution – Industry 4.0 – which, if not addressed, will add to a long list of ills, such as technological ills. There are strong correlations between the 21st-century skills needed to thrive in Industry 4.0 and early childhood cognitive, social and emotional, and language and communication development skills. Therefore, this book will cover the influencing factors that contribute to building exemplary citizenship and future leaders of the 21st century.

Being a visual person, having digested all the information that I've read and researched, I created a graphic to describe my vision for this book and subsequent resources to my family after some intense months of iterations. This is the first draft visual (mind-map) you see on the second page of this book (which will be expanded upon further). To my amazement, my family understood it and thought it was a good idea to pursue it further. I also knew that in our busy life and short attention span, any information presented should be in a powerful and straightforward format. I hope I have achieved this. Furthermore, I also made it a point to include and reference the research conducted by various scholars, scientists, and thought leaders to support the importance further.

This book poses the question, "Is it possible to hardwire the key skills that form the foundation or strong building blocks needed to produce exemplary future citizens that are conscientious, the best version of themselves, and have a strong desire to know, learn, and commit to lifelong learning continuously?"

This book explores the concept and provides the essential techniques and resources needed to hardwire these critical skills versus rewiring the skills at a later stage in life. Essentially, it provides an alternative, proactive approach that should be implemented before an individual experiences failure, has health issues, or has other life-changing experience that forces them to realize there is an issue with how they have lived their lives up until that point. There is evidence of how we often try to change our ways later in life. One common example is the typical billion-dollar industry of weight loss. Many health professionals tout this as simply having the discipline to eat healthily and follow a moderate exercise regimen, but most people cannot do that. Why is this? Keep reading, and I'll explain the root cause and potential remedies.

I sincerely hope that everyone that reads this book, in addition to shaping a better future for their young ones, can also personally benefit from a journey of self-improvement. I would also love to hear your thoughts and experiences as you apply the principles highlighted in this book. I had a lot of fun writing the book. I always felt positively energized as the dots got more explicit in my quest to "connect the dots" the deeper I looked. I also hope that every family across the globe can get access to this knowledge and hope we can resolve the "ills" that we see in the world right now. Collectively, as a society, we are moving towards a progressively worse situation. I am deeply blessed to be able to offer these resources as my humblest contribution to humanity and society in general. I am forever grateful!

Table of Contents

INTRODUCTION

<u>My Upbringing</u>

I was the youngest of 6 children; 3 boys and 3 girls. I was the stereotypical brat, but then I benefited greatly from the lessons learned from being part of a big family. Being the youngest, I experienced bullying from my oldest sibling. I often had to make do with hand-me-downs, but I could get away with mischief, and I got to do things earlier than my older siblings were typically allowed. My childhood, in a nutshell, was very happy. It was filled with adventure and discovery through hands-on, real-life experience. I grew up in an environment that was rich in learning and exploration, and I was surrounded by people who would serve as crucial role models for the entirety of my life. In short, "the world was my oyster." I felt I could achieve anything I wished for in life or go anywhere because I had the opportunity or ability to do so. It was so awesome that even today, I tell the younger generation to enjoy their youth instead of rushing to become adults, primarily because I sincerely believe that every phase of life has its joys. Still, the foundation for continued happiness and child-like enthusiasm in adult life starts with what's imprinted or hardwired in your younger years.

This description of my childhood might suggest I was uncommonly lucky to be in such an ideal environment, so let me explain further. I grew up in a middle-income family in Malaysia. My dad was the only breadwinner, and my mom was a homemaker. There were a total of 8 of us living in a 2-bedroom home. I don't recall having a dining room table until I was in my early teens. All six children would sit on the floor and form an assembly line where mom would serve us food, mainly to ensure she could regulate the servings and ensure everyone was fed. I also recall vividly that my mom would raise chickens and use the eggs from the chicken to barter for bread with the local baker, or bread man as we used to call him in Malaysia. Hopefully, you get the picture. I grew up with very modest means, but we had lots of love, and our home was filled with happiness, laughter, and adventure, especially with my partner in crime – my older brother. I would be remiss if I didn't acknowledge my brother Sam, two years older than me. He was and still is a significant influence and role model, and he was an intrinsic part of the adventure-seeking escapades we were involved in when we were younger.

My Belief Systems

Despite our modest means during my early childhood, the belief system that was imparted to me was very positive and impactful. But let's back up a little; what are belief systems? Essentially, they are principles or tenets that help us interpret our everyday reality. They include moral codes, spirituality, and philosophy. More importantly, these beliefs

2

are influenced and shaped by several factors. Belief systems and how they are shaped and influenced are an integral part of this book and will be explored.

I was fortunate to be surrounded by incredible role models; my mom and dad, my oldest sister Jyothi, who I affectionately called "Akka," and my partner in crime, and my older brother, Sam. Most of the moral codes that shaped my belief system came from my mom and dad. I learned to respect every human being, regardless of age, race, religion, or gender. I learned to love and be loved, be kind, and openly give to those less fortunate. I am not just talking about giving financial aid; I am also talking about giving your time as a volunteer, helping people with tasks, or simply making time to listen to another person's problems.

Many of the thoughts and feelings that formed part of my belief system were highly influenced by my sister, Jyothi, and my brother, Sam. They instilled in me the quality of discipline and the quality of being conscientious. This included the importance of giving a hundred percent on every task that I embarked on, the importance of learning from my mistakes and 'failing forward,' being confident and unafraid to experiment, and being fearless (the fearless part got me into some sticky situations, but there were rich lessons learned from it). They also instilled the value of always having a positive mindset (which is one of the key ingredients for having a growth mindset), always being enthusiastic, and having a strong desire to know and learn something new. In addition, they always encouraged me to be curious and innovative by figuring out why certain things work the way they do and how I could improve on them. My kids still joke about this today; they tell others, "If you want my dad to do something that he has not done before, all you have to do is challenge him to do it." I never back down from a challenge or having to figure things out, as long as it is not "insane or harmful to self or others." As a child, the curiosity instilled in me is still very much a part of my character.

In summary, they instilled in me the mindset that I can achieve anything I desire in life, especially if I am willing to put in the effort to succeed, learn from my mistakes, adapt, be persistent in my actions and follow-through, innovate, and pursue lifelong learning via curiosity constantly.

Other experiences that shaped my memories in my early childhood, and enriched and influenced my belief systems, came from outside my core family members. It was in the form of "hands-on play," interacting and communicating with others, playing games, exploring, reasoning, evaluating, problem-solving, and predicting. A target-rich environment allowed this exploration, manipulation, and development, which further influenced and shaped my belief system.

My First-Hand Experience & Knowledge Gained from the Corporate World

When I was 22 years old, I left Malaysia and headed to the United States to pursue my higher education. I earned a BS in Computer Science and entered the workforce. After my first five years in a non-management role in corporate America, I progressed into management and various executive positions. Along the way, I received an MBA and a Ph.D. by studying while I was working.

During my 30-year tenure in the corporate workplace, one of the areas I was responsible for as a manager and executive was developing the workforce into a high-performing one. One of the core responsibilities of a people manager is to conduct staff performance evaluations in a quarterly or annual performance management review process. A natural method of this exercise is to provide a performance rating and evaluate whether the individual exceeds, meets, or does not meet the performance expectations based on some agreed-upon or mandated performance metrics. In some cases, you would also have to stack-rank your employees and determine who the top 10% of the performers are and who gets the dubious "honor" of being in the bottom 10%. In my personal experience, having done hundreds of these performance reviews personally and approving reviews done by my managers, there was always a common theme that repeatedly appeared among the low performers, which I will address in the next section.

These themes were discovered as a result of asking probing questions, such as: (i) Are they willing to change? (ii) Do they even care? (iii) Are they motivated to change? (iv) Are they coachable? As you can see from these questions, they are all specific to the individual's willingness and abilities.

Most managers would start assessing the low-performers or non-performers on knowledge, skills, and the environment they are in. They would suggest using available remedies such as skills training (technical and soft skills) and opportunities to gain knowledge to improve their performance, but this does not fix the core issues within the individual. This provoked my further curiosity, and I explored why these common themes occur.

A quick note on skills training; currently, there is more focus on the soft skills training required for the individual to be at the desired performance level. In fact, with the current Industrial (Digital) Revolution (Industry 4.0), there is a strong emphasis for the workforce to excel in these soft skills that are part of the 21st-century skills to be high-performing. These are skills categorized as cognitive, intrapersonal, and interpersonal skills, with a more significant focus on soft skills training. More to come on this later.

My Curiosity & Quest for the Root Cause

My curiosity to explore the root causes of why these low performers are unwilling to change, do not care, or are unmotivated and not coachable, led me to "peel the onion." The curiosity to learn about - and truly understand - how these lower-performing individuals are wired led me to their belief systems. These belief systems were shaped and influenced during their early childhood and their life experiences.

This inquiry and search led me to uncover the common themes that led to their early childhood. One of the top-emerging themes was an inadequacy or lack of proper nurturing in the environment they grew up in. In some cases, childhood trauma causes negative emotional and psychological influences, resulting in negative belief systems. Beliefs such as, "You are not smart enough, and you will never amount to anything," and the lack of a positive role model, care, and compassion. These result in low self-esteem, lack of confidence, stress and anxiety, fear of failure, and many other ills. These are critical obstacles to functioning well. They're often self-imposed by adults due to past negative emotional and psychological experiences that impair cognitive, social, and emotional development.

I'll go over the importance of early childhood development stages, their correlation, and their impact on adult life separately. Still, I wanted to highlight the early revelations of the root cause analysis. A root cause analysis started with a simple interrogation technique of repeating the question, "Why?" This was followed by a deeper analysis of the answers that led me to further research on science and other evidence-based research explaining the causes, which compelled me to write this book.

Root cause analysis, if you are not familiar, is typically conducted to trace a problem to its origins. The issues I wish to discuss in this book are the societal, economic, and political ills that currently exist and seem to be escalating late. I plan to discuss the issues evident in the workforce, especially concerning underperforming employees and their unwillingness to change, their lack of engagement, motivation, and resistance to coaching and self-improvement. After identifying the "problems," this book attempts to show data that validates the fact that these problems genuinely exist, how long they have been in existence, and their impact. Once the above steps are explored, we then proceed to the final two phases of the root cause analysis - exploring why the causal factor exists and the real reason the problems occurred.

This will be followed by recommended solutions to help reduce the likelihood of these problems occurring and persisting through adulthood.

My Hope (Connecting the dots)

I hope you keep an open mind as you read and take a deeper dive with me into some well-researched explanations provided by world-renowned experts referenced in this book. My goal was to connect the dots in a simple, straightforward way to highlight the key actions and corrections that can be made to hardwire the proper skill set and belief system that influences the majority of steps we take as adults. Also, suppose you are an adult in the rewiring stage and are currently navigating and leveraging the massive resources available to improve a specific skill set that is deficient. In that case, you can learn how to accelerate the process by starting with the right mindset and understanding the root cause, as explained in this book.

As I mentioned earlier, this book started as a reference manual for a series of children's books – more on this later. It is up to you to take responsibility - especially if you are a parent, caregiver, or educator - and leverage the simple yet effective techniques provided in this book. It is essential to take the critical steps to help shape, nurture, and hardwire the vital and foundational skills needed to develop the cognitive, social, emotional, language, and communication skills during early childhood that will pay dividends in the future; steps that will reinforce the suitable belief systems and skillsets needed and will play a key role in helping build exemplary citizens and successful future leaders of the 21st-century.

Chapter 1: Current Worldwide Ills

<u>We Live in a World Full of Upheavals</u>

If you take a quick look around the world, there are so many upheavals, most commonly brought to the public's attention through the various demonstrations that are taking place around the globe; demonstrations that are both peaceful and violent and widely communicated through media channels. Furthermore, suppose you look at the underlying root cause for most of these demonstrations. In that case, it has to do with opposition to the "democratic deficit" that exists due to perceived or actual social, economic, or political situations viewed as uneven.

These demonstrations of opposition and dissent seem to be growing and can be seen worldwide at an increasing rate. This begs the question, "Why has there been such a dramatic increase in this type of dissent?" If we were to look deeper into each of the social, economic, and political deficits that cause dissent, we could probably find many reasons why these are occurring. However, a fascinating observation here, which seems to be a common thread among these demonstrations, is that it can unite and polarize different population segments, depending on their own biases and belief systems. It is important to note that it becomes systemic when bias is built into a system of belief, behavior, governance, business, or technology.

Systemic bias comes in many forms; overt discrimination, also known as macroaggression, or microaggressions, which are subtle, intentional, or unintentional interactions or behaviors that communicate some bias toward historically marginalized groups. I got my first-hand experience of microaggression when I moved to the U.S. back in 1985. My college mates and my host family would comment on my lack of an accent or how well I speak English. I dismissed this comment as ignorance on the part of my host family, but one could easily be offended because it could be viewed as discriminatory. Another excellent example between microaggression and microaggression was when one of my co-workers commented, "Wow, the audio does not match the video," meaning I did not sound the way I looked. A key distinction here is that the aggression may be displayed overtly or covertly, and the intent of the words or actions may be intentional or unintentional.

Regardless of the type of aggression, it has adverse social, emotional, psychological, and physical consequences for society. This particular subject of aggression is now more critical than ever, given the increase in a global workforce that is ethnically and gender diverse and multigenerational. As workplaces become more diverse, cultural sensitivity becomes more essential. Corporations must also focus more on bridging gaps through various cross-cultural sensitivity training and ramping up hiring through formalized diversity and inclusion programs.

Relevance to Early Childhood Development

Bias - regardless of the type of bias - can be curtailed at a very young age by teaching young children to understand and accept differences. Educators can play an important role here by creating a community that supports all dimensions of human differences, including culture, race, language, ability, learning styles, ethnicity, family structure, religion, sexual orientation, gender, age, and socioeconomic differences. Parents also have a critical role here; they must create an environment for their children that encourages the formation of strong, positive self-images and teaches them to respect and get along with people who are different from themselves.

Research has shown that children between 2 and 5 start becoming aware of gender, race, ethnicity, and disabilities (Neugebauer, 1992). They easily and quickly absorb both the positive attitudes and negative biases attached to these aspects of identity held by their family members and other significant adults in their lives. This is critical because this is what forms the unconscious bias that exists in each of us. It consists of the feelings, thoughts, urges, and memories outside our conscious awareness, created and stored in our unconscious mind, and are a product of all experiences since early childhood.

Obesity and Cancer

Obesity is a chronic disease affecting approximately 100 million adults in the U.S. Furthermore, according to the Centers for Disease Control and Prevention (CDC), about 40% of all cancers diagnosed in the U.S. have been associated with obesity and can cause other complications such as metabolic syndrome, high blood pressure, atherosclerosis, heart disease, diabetes, high blood cholesterol, and sleep disorders (National Heart, Lung and Blood Institute). Many factors cause obesity, and it is essential to note that some causes are easily controllable, like the balance of food intake and physical activity, managing stress, balanced emotion, and good sleep habits, to name a few. Citing the CDC *again, seven out of 10 U.S. deaths are caused by chronic disease. At the same time, roughly half of the country's population has been diagnosed with a chronic illness, including heart disease, cancer, diabetes, AIDS, or other conditions classified by the medical community as preventable. Let me repeat, "preventable."*

In today's environment, both healthcare providers and insurance companies focus on prevention strategies that have resulted in numerous programs. These include lifestyle coaches and group-based intervention programs that promote healthy eating, physical activity, stress management, etc. The global preventive healthcare technologies and services market is expected to reach $432.4

billion by 2024, according to a new report by Grand View Research, Inc. So, the obvious question is, "Why don't individuals have the discipline to cultivate these "good" habits on their own?" They have been recommended and proven by physicians as preventative measures that would diminish the onslaught of these diseases. *To begin answering this question, it is essential to understand what habits are and why these detrimental habits are so dominant in our lives.*

The author of the book "Better Than Before: Mastering the Habits of Our Everyday Lives," Gretchen Rubin, states *that habits are the invisible architecture of daily life.* I love this statement. Architecture is the art and science of designing and building essential ingredients for forming the foundation that allows you to create any final product. This foundation is in the background and invisible. She states that if we change our habits (the invisible architecture), we change our lives. And in her book, she provides some instructions on how you can potentially cultivate new, good habits. However, the excellent question is, how can we develop these new habits early on in life and prevent the "bad" habits? So, in line with the hardwiring in the title of this book, my quest was to understand how this "invisible architecture of daily life" was imprinted on us in the first place. To know that, we need to understand what habits are.

The first critical insight from the research conducted by Szegedy-Maszak, states that *current scientific estimates are that some 95 percent of our brain activity is unconscious* (Szegedy-Maszak, 2005). This means 95 percent of who we are involves a set of *unconscious* habits and patterns, automatic body function, creativity, emotions, personality, beliefs and values, cognitive biases, and long-term memory.

Let me pause here for a brief discussion on consciousness. Essentially, there are three levels of human consciousness, as popularized by Sigmund Freud throughout the Western world at the turn of the 20th century. The first level of consciousness is known as the conscious state, which refers to our immediate awareness. A good example would be your everyday experience; you are currently using your conscious mind by reading or listening to this book. We absorb input from our senses, analyze the information, and then make decisions and take actions based on this information. The bottom line is, if we're aware of it, either in the front of our minds or the back, then it is in the conscious mind.

The second level of consciousness - **the subconscious** - is the storage point for all remembered experiences and recent memories needed for quick recall. Given that the subconscious holds every experience you've ever had, every thought, and every impression, it dramatically influences our patterns of thought and behavior. Our habits form patterns of thought and behavior over time. These habits are learned through practice and repetition until they lock into our subconscious minds and become a permanent part of our behavior. We do things so well that we do them without thinking; mental processes we initially use the conscious mind for, over an extended period, we delegate to the subconscious.

A good example would be, when we first learn to drive, we have to think about every action we take, and we become competent drivers when we pay conscious attention to what we're doing. Once we've been driving for many years, our mind offloads much of the work of driving safely to our subconscious mind. We become subconsciously competent at driving. An extreme example of the subconscious at work is when we get in the car to drive to work while being consciously aware of something other than driving. Often, we arrive at the workplace with no recollection of intentionally driving the vehicle from point A to B.

The final level of consciousness is known as the **unconscious**; this is where all our memories and experience reside. It is made up of thoughts, memories, and instinctual desires buried deep within ourselves but may sometimes be repressed through trauma. Even though we're not aware of their existence, they significantly influence our behavior. From these memories and experiences, our beliefs, habits, and behaviors are formed. Freud's "Iceberg Theory" uses the image of an iceberg to illustrate the three levels of consciousness. As most of you know, an iceberg only reveals a portion of its "true self" as it floats in the water with the remaining mass, which is considerably more prominent and more influential, concealed below the surface. Similarly, the conscious mind is what we freely reveal on a day-to-day basis in our interactions with others - the exposed part of the iceberg - while the more significant part of ourselves (the subconscious and unconscious) is deeply submerged and concealed - a part of us that no one gets to see. The exception to this is known as a "Freudian slip," where the emergence of an unconscious mind reveals the honest underlying thoughts and feelings people hold.

To conclude the topic of consciousness, it is essential to note that, although there is a direct link between the subconscious and unconscious, they deal with similar things. The unconscious mind is the vault containing all your memories, habits, and behaviors; a repository that has been programmed since birth and throughout our childhood with different memories and experiences (both good and bad) that form the habits, beliefs, fears, trust issues, curiosities and insecurities that drive our day-to-day behaviors.

Relevance to Early Childhood Development

Here, I would like to *re-emphasize my earlier point.* *95% of who we are consists of habitual unconscious thoughts and unconscious emotional reactions.* This is a crucial factor to remember, and it will be revisited later in this book. I hope you see the common thread about how these sets of habitual unconscious thoughts and unconscious emotional reactions can be programmed with the proper habits, beliefs, and stimuli as part of the early childhood development stages.

Poverty, Unemployment, and the Failing Education System

All three of these topics are very controversial. According to sociologists, they make up one's social class. More specifically, sociologists agree that *social class* - determined by education, income, occupational status, and wealth levels - impacts families and shapes their lives and opportunities; it defines their socioeconomic status.

It is widely known that low-income families have fewer material resources and opportunities and often live in more impoverished neighborhoods with fewer resources available and less desirable school districts. Several studies suggest that two main variables i.e., education level and parent's wealth have long lasting generational impact. Parents pass on social advantages or disadvantages. The parents' economic status determines the neighborhood they live in, and more excellent areas generate more significant local property taxes. In the United States and many other parts of the world, local schools are financed predominantly through local property taxes; thus, the more wealthy the area, the more resources available.

Furthermore, extensive research has demonstrated "that children's social class is one of the most significant predictors, if not the single most significant predictor of their educational success" (Garcia & Weiss, 2017). Our failing education system exacerbates this problem, especially in the United States, where inequities in school funding systems still exist. Despite the single-minded focus on raising achievement levels and closing socioeconomic gaps during the 'No Child Left Behind' era that spanned from 2002 until 2015.

The recent pandemic and closing of schools also revealed to many, including myself, that more than half of the children attending U.S. public schools qualify for free or reduced-price lunch. Thus, alternate means to provide these meals were needed due to the school closures. This is the highest statistic recorded since the National Center for Education Statistics began tracking this figure decades ago. Predictably, there is a domino effect whereby the lower social class gives rise to a lower education success rate, which contributes to a higher rate of unemployment due to lower education success. In a recent 2019 survey by the U.S. Department of Commerce, the unemployment rate was the highest for those who had just completed high school – 43%, and the lowest, at 13%, for those with a bachelor's or higher degree. This issue was also brought to light due to the COVID-19 pandemic, with the rising unemployment rate including a more extensive representation of people from a lower social class.

To highlight several factors, I have presented to you the issues surrounding social class and the downstream effect, the idea that social class can be passed down through generations. For example, the impact on early childhood development and how the influence of the environment that you grow up in shapes your product. Concerning early childhood development, children who grow up in a lower social class and attend schools with fewer and substandard resources will experience a direct negative impact on their cognitive, social and emotional, and language and communication skills development.

More broadly, poverty means deprivation for children that results in hunger, illness, insecurity, neglect, and instability – all of which causes increased stress and, in turn, impacts developmental outcomes.

With industry 4.0 and the advancement of automation and artificial intelligence, there will be a reduction in manual operations, and consequently, people engaged in blue-collar jobs will need to upskill. Through the infusion of artificial intelligence, robotics, and big data into the workplace, automation will elevate the demand for the current workforce to improve and add to their existing skill sets.

This will result in the new, blue-collar labor force requiring 21st-century skills such as complex reasoning, social and emotional intelligence, creativity, and certain forms of sensory perception, to name a few; skills that cannot be replaced through automation, but rather, skills required to constantly refine automation, thus requiring a renovation of their current skills. So, given that the environment plays a crucial role in future success, and there is a significant advancement of the digital industry 4.0, how can we hardwire these skills at an early age, and how do these skills help with the development of 21st-century skills? Keep reading, as the blueprint will be laid out here in this book.

Relevance to Early Childhood Development

Unfortunately, poverty is environmental adversity that is little affected by a child's actions. Being exposed to these adverse conditions for an extended period may result in children experiencing extreme stress, which in turn impacts and disrupts the development of the brain, and leads to impairment of cognitive, social, and emotional development (National Scientific Council on the Developing Child, 2005/2014).

Therefore, it is essential to equip caregivers with stress management techniques that they can utilize to prepare children growing up in these environments with coping mechanisms to minimize the negative impacts. There is also a direct correlation between early childhood development focused on social and emotional skills essential for the development of 21st-century skills.

Educators and government agencies are focusing more on these skills, and it has now evolved into one of the hottest early childhood development topics, called social and emotional learning (SEL). For those of you who have not heard about SEL, several frameworks are used to facilitate SEL. A common and popular framework is the Collaborative for Academic, Social, and Emotional Learning (CASEL). One of the most dominant frameworks in the field is the "CASEL five," consisting of five competencies. These five competencies are self-awareness, self-management, social awareness, relationship skills, and responsible decision-making. SEL, as published on the CASEL website, "is the process through which children and adults acquire and effectively apply the knowledge, attitudes, and skills necessary to understand and manage emotions, set and achieve positive goals, feel and show empathy for others, establish and maintain positive relationships, and make a responsible decision" (CASEL.org). I also have an incredible and beautiful resource that I stumbled upon as I was researching SEL, the Chooselovemovement.org. I will expand on this later in the book.

Chapter 2: Current Solutions and Its Challenges

Bridging the Democratic Deficit

We have briefly discussed the 'democratic deficit' in an earlier passage in this book. A "democratic deficit" is primarily due to perceived or actual social, economic, or political outcomes viewed as uneven. We also have various governmental checks and balances in place, working alongside many international organizations to protect against a democratic deficit. Here's a small sampling of these international organizations and a brief description of why they exist.

EUROPEAN UNION (EU) - The EU, in its preamble to its Charter of Fundamental Rights, states:

"The peoples of Europe, in creating an ever-closer union among them, are resolved to share a peaceful future based on common values. Conscious of its spiritual and moral heritage, the Union is founded on the indivisible, universal values of human dignity, freedom, equality, and solidarity; it is based on democracy and the rule of law."

It places the individual at the heart of its activities by establishing the citizenship of the Union and by creating an area of freedom, security, and justice. If you want to read the entire preamble, there is more to this, but you get the gist.

The INTERNATIONAL MONETARY FUND (IMF) - The IMF's website states:

"The International Monetary Fund (IMF) is an organization of 190 countries, working to foster global monetary cooperation, secure financial stability, facilitate international trade, promote high employment and sustainable economic growth, and reduce poverty worldwide."

The UNITED NATIONS (UN) - The UN's central mission is to maintain international peace and security by protecting human rights, delivering humanitarian aid, upholding international law, and promoting sustainable development. One of its main priorities is to "achieve international cooperation in solving international economic, social, cultural or humanitarian problems, and promote and encourage respect for human rights and fundamental freedoms for all, without distinction regarding race, gender, language or religion."

The WORLD TRADE ORGANIZATION (WTO) - The WTO is a global organization dealing with trade rules between nations. In its website, it has a booklet that states, "Ten things the WTO can do," and it includes items such as cutting living costs and rising living standards; settling disputes and reducing trade tensions; stimulating economic growth and employment; cutting the cost of doing business internationally; encouraging good governance; helping countries develop; giving the weak a more robust voice; supporting the environment and health; contributing to peace and stability, and being effective without hitting the headlines.

So, the million-dollar question - why is there a continuous rise in protests and resentment touting the democratic deficit when all these checks and balances are in place? A simple logical answer would be because it is a massive undertaking. There are many competing interests, value systems, desire to protect sovereignty and independence, inability to agree on maintaining the balance between market liberalization and social protection, and many other reasons.

Multiple sources talk about the various failures of these international organizations in curbing democratic deficits. Upon careful examination, you will see a common thread emerge, distinct from the disconnect between international and national policies, namely, the overly bureaucratic structure; greed; and bias - both conscious and unconscious bias - which is the same underlying factor that I highlighted earlier—systemic discrimination rooting back to our belief systems.

Treating the Symptoms versus the Root Cause

According to the Centers for Disease Control and Prevention, 90% of the nation's $3.5 trillion annual healthcare expenditure is for people with chronic and mental health conditions. With healthcare costs on the rise, and 51% of all mortality being directly attributable to lifestyle choices, people have more control over their health than they think.

For example, 85% of all type 2 diabetes diagnoses and the side effects are preventable (Mokdad et al., 2000). If this is the case, does it not make sense to move away from treating symptoms to finding and treating the root cause of disease, especially if these root causes are preventable?

One common complaint frequently heard about the U.S. healthcare system is that it is structured around diagnosis and treatment rather than wellness and prevention. We need to operate as a "health" care system versus working as a "sick" care system and focus more on ensuring that more individuals get the recommended primary and preventive care. It should be a more holistic approach since many chronic diseases are preventable through lifestyle choices or early detection and management of risk factors. Many can also be managed with medical treatment and improved diet and exercise.

The CDC lists the following items as the key risk factors for the rise in chronic disease: tobacco use, poor nutrition, lack of physical activity, and excessive alcohol use. All of these risk factors are preventable, but why do we continue with these lifestyles, and more importantly, what drives us (root cause) to continue with these harmful lifestyles if we know that they cause harm to us?

It is one thing for the U.S. healthcare system to educate us on preventive care. Still, each individual also needs to avoid smoking, eating unhealthy foods, excessive alcohol consumption, and living a sedentary lifestyle to improve overall well-being.

See the common theme here? Habits and behaviors! Billion-dollar industries have sprung up to educate the general public with various programs, plans, coaches, and other resources to help us live a healthy lifestyle and form new habits. However, the problem persists.

In reviewing the latest World Health Statistics (2020) published by the World Health Organization (WHO) on 3 of the critical risk factors, "obesity, in particular, is on the rise globally, and alcohol use is also increasing in some regions. Meanwhile, the decline in tobacco use is slowing." I have already touched on habits and behaviors, but let's look at other underlying causes that make these habits appear and persist.

One common root cause is stress - yes, stress. According to the WHO, stress has been classified as the health epidemic of the 21st century. This was proclaimed before the 2020 COVID-19 pandemic; now, one can only imagine the stress levels since the pandemic's onset.

Now, when I read this, I was surprised because I did not see the other "usual suspects" - smoking, eating unhealthy foods, excessive alcohol consumption, and living a sedentary lifestyle - on the list that classified the "health epidemic of the 21st century," even though, they are all considered key risk factors and the underlying root causes for the rise in chronic diseases. So, I decided to take a closer look into stress and found out that there have been rigorous studies conducted for the past decade on the relationship between stress and inflammation and its impact on our health.

As I was looking further into the studies on stress, I came across an article in Time Magazine's June 6, 1983 cover story naming stress "The Epidemic of the Eighties." referring to stress as our leading health problem – mind-blowing since this was almost 40 years ago, and it is the same today.

Studies suggest that chronic stress (stress that lasts for an extended period) negatively impacts our bodies' **inflammatory responses** (Cohen et al., 2002, 2012). There's evidence that the inflammatory response pathway is pivotal in the pathogenesis of many chronic diseases (Liu, Wang & Jiang, 2017). The "Inflammatory Response Pathway" is our immune system's response to harmful stimuli such as pathogens, infection, tissue damage, or toxic compounds and acts by removing harmful stimuli and initiating the healing process. 75% to 90% of human disease is related to stress and inflammation, including cardiovascular and metabolic diseases and neurodegenerative disorders (an illness that involves the death of certain parts of our brain -e.g., memory loss, as seen in Alzheimer's patients) (Liu et al., 2017).

Liu et al. also posit that research has shown that chronic stress, experienced in early life or as an adult, contributes to an increased risk of coronary heart disease.

A key point here is that stress experienced in early life is a contributing factor, and this was one of the many motivations for me to write this book. It is also important to note that chronic stress and inflammation also contribute to other illnesses such as depression, autoimmune diseases, upper respiratory infections, and poor wound healing (Cohen et al., 2010). Another fascinating study, which was published in 2019 in the Journal of Molecular Psychiatry, details how a team of researchers from Cambridge examined the link between depression and coronary heart disease and concluded with the findings that suggest the connection between these two conditions cannot be explained by a common genetic predisposition, but rather, it is environmentally related (Kandaker, 2019). This is an important finding that highlights the environmental impact and the role of epigenetics, which I will expand upon further in later chapters of the book. It also ties back to the need for the healthcare system to be more preventive and take a more holistic view of a person's health by looking at multiple factors together, for instance, heart disease and depression, primarily to gain a better understanding of how factors like traumatic experiences and the environmental impact one's physical and mental health.

In concluding the topic of treating the symptoms instead of the root cause and taking a holistic approach to healthcare, I wanted to highlight the proliferation of stress management resources available to you. At the time of writing, a quick Google search on "stress management" revealed 967 million potential resources for stress management. Despite the number of resources available to help with stress management, according to the WHO, stress is still considered a health epidemic of the 21st century.

Therefore, what I wanted to do in straightforward terms is to explain what stress is and how it has evolved. Hopefully, with this understanding, you can apply this knowledge to all the stressful episodes that you might encounter in your life and reduce the impact that they can have on your body if it is not managed. Additionally, this understanding would also be beneficial as you look into the various resources available to help you reduce your stress level and reduce the onslaught of mental health problems and other diseases.

There are two types of stress; acute stress (short-term) and chronic stress (that lasts for a more extended period). Everyone experiences acute stress at one time or another; for instance, when you see a police car with flashing lights in your rear-view mirror or when our ancestors had to evade dangerous animals to survive.

The stress response, typically called fight-flight-freeze, is not conscious. It is the body's natural response to danger and is triggered instantly, causing physiological and biochemical changes to kick in. These changes make your brain more alert, cause your muscles to tense, and are essentially your body's way of protecting itself. It affects your whole body; your heart beats faster to bring oxygen to your significant muscles; your lungs are impacted when your breathing speeds up, or you might hold your breath or restrict breathing; your blood thickens, which increases clotting factors to prepare your body for injury and other faculties as well. All of these are critical to survival when you are in danger.

On the other hand, chronic stress is the stress that lasts for an extended period, and if it persists for weeks and months, it may lead to serious health problems. It is also equally important to note that these physiological reactions, specifically when it comes to acute stress, are triggered by a psychological fear, and this fear is conditioned. This means you've associated fear with negative experiences. The psychological response is initiated when you're first exposed to the situation, and it then develops over time. A key point here is that the negative experience or trauma is embedded in your subconscious, which becomes habitual. The same behavioral and physiological response will repeatedly occur when perceived or real danger.

Not all negative experiences are bad, but they are necessary for survival; for instance, millions of years ago, our ancestors ran away from their prey to survive. *However, what we have created in our current multitasking life, competing to be the best, being perfectionists, etc., is self-induced stress. As a result, most stressors are triggered by our daily actions and behaviors.* This leads to chronic stress that extends over a long period and is harmful to your health-related chronic diseases.

To explain this further, our body, at an intrinsic level, consists of two separate protection systems, namely, growth and protection, which are critical for maintaining life. Development is essential for our overall well-being. Every day, billions of cells in our body wear out and need to be replaced. In protection mode, especially when there is an external threat, the various physiological and biochemical changes launch the body's organs into action for survival. So,

33

acute stress, like in a fight-or-flight response, impacts the growth systems because the energy responsible for the growth of cells and the production of the body's energy reserves is redirected to enhance our physiological power to fend off or flee from danger. If our growth and protection/immune systems are suppressed for an extended period due to our self-induced stress, it becomes chronic. It could lead to depression, mood disorders, and other chronic diseases.

This leads me to the next point about the vagus nerve. I would be remiss if I didn't include a brief discussion about the vagus nerve, your secret weapon in fighting stress. The vagus nerve serves as the superhighway. It is one cranial nerve that connects the brain to the body. It carries information between the brain and the internal organs and controls the body's response during relaxation times. The measure of how strong your vagus nerve is (called the vagal tone) can be connected to inflammation, immune system regulation, metabolism, and emotional regulation. It is a significant part of how our bodies and brains function. We can receive powerful health benefits if we know how to stimulate it, especially during chronic stress. Having a higher vagal tone means your body can relax faster after stress.

There are many self-help exercises that can help stimulate your vagus nerve for you to choose from, and you can also find more resources on how this is part of your parasympathetic (rest and digest) nervous system. One way to stimulate the healthy functions of the vagus nerve is through deep, slow belly breathing.

I have endeavored to describe what stress is and how it is part of your subconscious and self-induced (I will cover this in more detail in 'influencing early life experiences as a caregiver and educator to young children'). Additionally, I've also stressed the importance of managing self-induced stress and talked about the vagus nerve as a secret weapon that you can tap into to minimize chronic stress. You will see a strong parallel here if you notice what I mentioned earlier about your belief systems. While positive perceptions or beliefs enhance health by engaging the immune systems, negative perceptions or beliefs lead to stress, will eventually inhibit the immune activities, and can lead to chronic disease. In summary, prevention is far cheaper and more effective than treatment after the fact; however, changing health-related behaviors is difficult, as illustrated above. Again, the key culprits are those darn habits that are the "invisible architects of your daily life" and are part of your subconscious mind, not to mention the equally influential environmental factors, which will be covered later when I discuss the topic of epigenetics.

Relevance to Early Childhood Development

As you can see, the underlying "usual suspects" are the belief systems, habits, and environmental influence. All these factors are rooted at an early age. They can be easily shaped and nurtured with a healthy environment, set of practices, and belief systems to develop early childhood cognitive, social and emotional, and language and communication skills.

How effective would it be if we were to teach individuals the "how-to" at an early age instead of allowing them to form bad habits and belief systems? A simple "how-to" on how to handle stress would greatly benefit the prevention of chronic diseases, but we are not taught any techniques when we are growing up. In my professional life, I was told "to suck it up" and "be a man" if I was in hyper or constant stress. Meanwhile, I would have benefited if someone had told me how to activate my vagus nerve by breathing to minimize my stress level.

Stress can also lead to social isolation and loneliness, and research has also shown that stress due to social isolation is more potent and an underestimated risk factor. A UCLA epigeneticist stated that social isolation is the best-established, more robust social and psychological risk factor contributing to diseases (Cole et al., 1996). Where does the social insecurity that leads to social isolation and loneliness come from, and how can we remedy it? Is it possible to fix this during the development of social and emotional skills in early childhood? Short answer – yes. And a topic that is gaining much popularity is social and emotional learning (SEL), which is being embraced as a potential remedy.

21st Century Skills Readiness

I touched on this briefly but want to expand further on what '21st-century skills' means and why it is something that you should pay attention to - or at least be aware of. A key component of 21st-century skills is the personal and academic competencies required for success in the 21st-century society and workplace. Since the early 1980s, governmental, corporate, and educational institutions have focused on this. It originated in the U.S. and eventually spread to other nations globally with the help of national and international organizations such as the Asia-Pacific Economic Cooperation (APEC) and the Organization for Economic Co-operation and Development (OECD). Predictably, it resulted in many definitions of these skills and competencies by the different bodies.

In 2012, the U.S. National Research Council of the National Academies (NRC) published a paper titled, 'Education for Life and Work: Developing Transferable Knowledge and Skills in the 21st Century' (NRC, 2012) as a first step toward describing 21st-century skills that are now widely recognized. The NRC reviewed and incorporated all previous efforts to identify these competencies and came up with three domains of competency that included distinct facets of human thinking, human development, and learning, namely: **cognitive, intrapersonal, and interpersonal.**

So, let's unpack each of these competencies and look at how well-equipped our education system and corporations are in arming our students and the workforce to be competent in these skills and thrive in the 21st-century industry 4.0.

Cognitive competencies consist of three main areas: cognitive processes and strategies, knowledge, and creativity. Essentially, they are skills associated with acquiring knowledge and processing information through thought, such as reasoning, intuition, perception, imagination, innovation, creativity, problem-solving, active listening, and oral and written expression.

Intrapersonal competencies include intellectual openness, work ethic/conscientiousness, and positive core self-evaluation. Skills associated with adaptability, self-management, self-development, and self-awareness help control your attitudes and inner processes. They form the foundation for relationship building and help navigate your interpersonal relationships.

Finally, **interpersonal competencies** consist of teamwork, collaboration, and leadership; primarily, behaviors, tactics, and traits you rely on when you interact and communicate with others in various scenarios where communication and cooperation are essential.

Now that you have a good understanding of 21st-century skills, let's explore how our education system equips our youth with these skills and the competency level in the corporate workforce.

Workforce Readiness

The Fourth Industrial Revolution – Industry 4.0 – had a dominating and far-reaching impact on the future of work and the skills that are needed for the workforce. A recent study by the Global McKinsey Institute states that by 2030, with the rise of automation and artificial intelligence (A.I.), as many as 375 million workers globally will have to upskill, as their current jobs would evolve to work alongside capable machines (Manyika et al., 2019). In a rapidly advancing, technology-driven world, the report states that by 2020, 50% of companies believe that automation will decrease their reliance and need for full-time staff, and by 2030 robots will potentially replace about 800 million workers worldwide. These figures are at an estimated 47 percent of U.S. jobs potentially displaced over the next 20 years with automation and the rapid advances in A.I., cognitive computing, and automation of repetitive tasks (Frey & Osborne, 2013). All critical data points requiring substantial workplace transformations and changes for all workers in the U.S. and globally in reskilling and upskilling.

I wanted to take a quick pause to explain the difference between reskilling and upskilling since, although they both require the process of learning new skills, there is a difference. Reskilling starts with identifying your current workforce with adjacent skills that are close to the unique abilities the organization requires. According to the World Economic Forum, 54 percent of all employees will require significant reskilling by 2022. On the other hand, Upskilling teaches employees new and advanced skills to close the talent gap, typically suitable for employees with deep knowledge and experience in the organization's internal workings, culture, and customers.

The essential data point here is that both reskilling and upskilling require the right mindset and willingness to learn, hence the importance of instilling lifelong learning habits early on in youth or during early childhood development stages.

According to a recent survey conducted on Global Skills Shortage by the Society for Human Resource Management (SHRM, 2018), 83% of the respondents cited difficulties hiring suitable candidates over 12 months because of the lack of the desired skills needed for the position. Furthermore, 75% of those having difficulty recruiting stated a shortage in skills among their applicants, both in technical skills and soft skills. Among the top missing soft skills, in rank order, were: problem-solving: critical thinking: innovation and creativity, ability to deal with complexity and ambiguity, and the last missing skill being communication. What is more troubling with this survey result is that over 50% of respondents feel the skills shortage has worsened in their organization in the last two years and that the education systems have done little or nothing to help address the skills deficiency – ouch!

The soft skills training market has ballooned in growth worldwide as more and more organizations are leveraging these resources to bridge the soft skills gap in their workforce. According to a recent report on Global Soft Skills Industry by Reportlinker.com (2020), the global market for soft skills training in 2020 is estimated to be $229.6 million and could potentially reach $347.8 million by 2027. Next, we will delve into another example of multiple resources and industries emerging to solve problems that could have been solved upstream by other resources and entities like the education system.

Education System Readiness

In exploring the current education system, and if I were to give an overall letter grade on how well we are preparing our youth with the essential 21st-century skills, I would probably say a "C." After reading what I discovered, some of you might provide an overall grade of "F."

The disparity in the availability and access to resources across the globe is a huge factor. Still, there are pockets of encouraging efforts and progress, and I'm also an optimist, hence an overall grade of "C-." It truly "takes a village" to get this on the right trajectory.

Let's take a more in-depth look at the statistics. In 2015, the United Nations adopted the Sustainable Development Goals (SDGs), comprising 17 interlinked goals designed to be a blueprint for achieving a better and more sustainable global future for all by 2030. Goal number 4 out of the 17 goals was to provide Quality Education to 262 million children and adolescents out of school in 2015. The specific target was to ensure that all girls and boys complete accessible, equitable, and quality primary and secondary education, leading to relevant learning outcomes. In reviewing the UN SDG progress report, it stated that it was not on track to meet the 2030 education goal targets, and this was before the 2020 COVID-19 pandemic; currently, this pandemic has only made the situation even worse.

In the U.S., you can review the National Assessment of Education Progress (NAEP) report cards for many statistics on how the nation is fairing in preparing our youth. In summary – "not well." I refer to a press conference given in October 2020 by the U.S. Secretary of Education that made a statement on the new reading and mathematics results for 12th-grade students on the "The Nation's Report Card." Here's the exact quote from Betsy DeVos (former Secretary of Education):

"Sadly, today's results confirm America's schools continue to fall far short and fail too many kids, especially the most disadvantaged. Being a high school graduate should mean something. But when 40% of these graduates are 'below basic' in math, and 30% are 'below basic' in reading, it's hard to argue that the education system is preparing them for what comes next."

All of these statistics are readily available for the public to view. The latest figures on the total expenditure for public elementary and secondary education were for 2018 and totaled $739 billion. "Falling short" were the words of the former U.S. Secretary of Education, despite an increase in spending for six consecutive years and a total 2018 expenditure of $739 billion.

This theme of falling short continues with higher education and high school graduates that make the transition to colleges and universities. The U.S. Department of Education reported that the overall 6-year graduation rate for first-time, full-time undergraduate students who began seeking a bachelor's degree at 4-year degree-granting institutions was 62 percent. That means over a third of the students who enrolled in college still haven't earned a bachelor's degree at the six-year mark. As for the 62 percent that eventually graduate, and based on recent data published in 2020 by the Federal Reserve Bank of New York, 41 percent of recent college graduates and 33.8 percent of all college graduates are underemployed and working in jobs that don't require a college degree.

So, in summary, the education system "as is" needs reform. It also highlights that obtaining an education beyond high school is no longer a luxury but rather a necessity for most to maintain a decent quality of life. According to the U.S. Bureau of Labor Statistics, the recent 2020 pandemic exposed the fractures in the education system with the highest unemployment rate since the Great Depression, among those that had less than a high school diploma, followed by high school graduates. Jobs that only require a high school diploma are fading away. For the U.S. or any other nation to maintain its competitiveness globally, the ability to access and complete a high-quality post-secondary education or even a certificate-granting institution has never been more critical.

Furthermore, it is no surprise to anyone that the world we live and work in is changing at a rapid pace, fueled by a fast-paced development in technology impacting the global job market. Also, the Institute for the Future (IFTF) (Manyika et al., 2019), an institute that identifies emerging trends and their impacts on global society, forecasts that up to 85 percent of the jobs that today's college students will hold in 2030 don't exist right now. If the IFTF's forecast is accurate, then the critical question is, how can schools worldwide prepare today's students for tomorrow's workplace?

The World Economic Forum report states that over 50% of the workforce will require significant reskilling, and we would be naïve not to observe that the global job market has been progressively changing at a much faster pace since the invention of the World Wide Web in 1989, Wi-Fi in 1997 and then the smartphone in 2007. Over 18 years, we went from the dawn of the World Wide Web to the iPhone. Emerging and future technologies continue to evolve exponentially with artificial intelligence, robotics, the internet of things (IoT), 3D printing, and many more innovations.

The key challenge here is that the world is not static. We have no idea what new piece of technology will drive and drastically change the world economy, hence the importance of preparing our students for a dynamic world with jobs, opportunities, and challenges that do not yet exist.

Educators need to shift from focusing on curriculum, rote memorization, and administering test problems with known answers to teaching students how to come up with multiple solutions to open-ended, unscripted problems. It is these types of open-ended and complex problems they will face as they pursue future careers. The emphasis should be on skills and competencies, instead of curriculum and rote memorization, which many educators and education systems still rely on as the standard to teach our students.

A quick explanation of the difference between skills and competencies. Skills are learned abilities required to perform a particular task successfully, whereas competencies are knowledge and behaviors that lead you to success in your role. The shift is necessary because technological advances, like the internet and smartphone, have rendered skills like rote memorization unimportant; instead, students should be taught how to retrieve, synthesize, think critically, and evaluate the vast library of information found online. This further emphasizes the importance of a curriculum that focuses on fostering 21st-century skills that include - but are not limited to - digital literacy, problem-solving, collaboration, creativity, reasoning, synthesizing, and analysis to help the student prepare for a multitude of situations they will encounter as they pursue their future career.

Relevance to Early Childhood Development

Going back to my earlier statement that it "takes a village" for reform to be successful, it is essential for a parent, caregiver, educator, or anyone in an influential role to take action and contribute to effective change. It may be participating in a cause like the SDG, creating awareness of the dire need for reform, or selecting and voting for the right leaders in your nation that understand and are willing to impact change for the better in this arena. My form of contribution is through this book. There is a strong parallel between the 21st-century skills described above and children's early childhood development skills: cognitive skills, language and communication, and social and emotional skills.

The building blocks or the foundation needed for healthy development and execution of 21st-century skills start with nurturing and developing the early childhood development skills. Unfortunately, this one simple but obvious fact is overlooked and marginalized by other perceived priorities.

Although efforts to shape and nurture these skills early on with our youth are gaining popularity, it is not widespread, holistic, or fully realized how powerful this could be as a significant contributing factor for building exemplary citizenship and 21st-century future leaders that are conscientious and compassionate. Chapter 3 will give you the details on this alternative, proactive, impactful, and sustainable solution.

Chapter 3: An Alternative Proactive and Complementary Solution

A Quick Recap

I have provided a brief overview of some worldwide ills, the increase in chronic diseases and poverty, unemployment, and the failing education system. I have also offered a sampling of the current "solutions" provided by various governmental and international organizations and their lack of progress and continuous challenges. I have also exposed some of the significant common themes that emerged. Each one of these ills and shortcomings centered around the themes of systemic bias, habits, and belief systems via the influence of the subconscious mind and the environment. Finally, I've highlighted the importance of developing 21st-century skills to succeed in the current industry 4.0 and how there is a strong correlation between the development of early childhood development skills and its importance in building 21st-century skills. This is just a brief overview of each topic since I could write several books.

My goal here is to give you enough knowledge and enable you to see the connections and root causes that can be potentially fixed upstream. More importantly, the shortcomings of the current solutions in place leading up to the importance of this chapter of the book — an understanding of the importance of your role as a parent, caregiver, or educator responsible for developing skills in young children. I sincerely believe that this understanding and willingness to commit to developing these skills well during early childhood will pay dividends later on in life in the form of creating exemplary citizenship and 21st-century future leaders.

The Resemblance

In Chapter 2, I described the three keys of 21st-century skills, namely, cognitive, intrapersonal, and interpersonal skills. I also explained how organizations globally are challenged to ramp up their current workforce with these skills, either through reskilling or upskilling. So, given these challenges, is there an alternative or complementary solution in addition to the plethora of resources that have emerged over the years to help bridge this gap?

This is where I make a case for the strong influence of early childhood development skills helping with the advancement of 21st-century skills by hardwiring the correct abilities, disciplines, and behaviors from the day a child is born or even while the baby is in the mother's womb.

A child develops in specific, predictable ways - which are referred to as the developmental milestones - and they explain how they learn and grow. According to the CDC, milestones cover four areas of child development. They are cognitive, communication and language, social and emotional, and motor. At a very high level, motor development means the physical growth and strengthening of a child's bones, muscles, and ability to move and touch his/her surroundings. The main emphasis in this section of the book will be the first three – cognitive, communication and language, and social and emotional.

Cognitive skills describe the core skills your brain uses to explore, learn, think and figure out how to solve problems. Cognitive skills include attention, short-term memory, long-term memory, logic and reasoning, auditory processing, visual processing, and processing speed. They take incoming information and move it into the bank of knowledge used every day at school, at work, and in life.

To truly understand the development of cognitive abilities in children, we have to discuss The Theory of Cognitive Development, written by one of the most significant researchers in developmental psychology of the 20th century – Jean Piaget. Piaget's theory is known as 'the development stage theory' and suggests that children move through four different stages of mental development. According to Piaget, these stages are:

• **Sensorimotor Stage:** Birth through about two years. During this earliest stage of cognitive development, children learn about the world and acquire knowledge through their senses and manipulating objects – essentially, basic reflexes, senses, and motor responses. Growth and learning occur in this stage through active interaction with their environment and making discoveries, learning about language from people they interact with, and performing physical actions such as crawling and walking. This is the stage where they also develop an early representation of thought; when a child can picture something in their mind and object permanence; when a child realizes that an object exists even if they can't see or touch it (a game of peek-a-boo helps develop object permanence). This allows a child to learn that objects are separate and distinct entities and that they have their existence outside their perception. This is an important milestone. The infant lives in the present and does not have a mental picture of the world stored in its memory, nor does it have object permanence at the beginning of this stage – a critical point that I will revisit later.

● **Preoperational Stage:** Ages 2 through 7. During this stage, children develop memory and imagination and understand the ideas of the past and future. They know things symbolically – the ability to make one thing, such as a word or an object, stand for something other than itself. Infants at this stage also demonstrate animism - the tendency to think that non-living things (such as toys) have life and feel like a person. The critical milestone here is the use of language that becomes more mature and thoughtful – although, at this stage, thinking is based on intuition and is still not entirely logical.

- **Concrete Operational Stage:** Ages 7 through 11. During this stage, children become more aware of external events and feelings other than their own. They become less selfish and begin to understand that not everyone shares their thoughts, beliefs, or feelings. This stage is called concrete because children can think logically and much more successfully if they can manipulate actual (concrete) materials or pictures of them. It marks the beginning of logical or operational thought.

- **Formal Operational Stage:** Ages 11 and older. Children can use logic to solve problems, view the world around them, and plan for the future during this stage.

Now that you understand Piaget's theory, I want to stress that this is one of many theories that developmental psychologists have proffered to understand the nature and sources of growth in children's cognitive, language, and social skills. This controlled growth is an everyday theoretical basis for psychologists. It underscores the contribution of both biology and the environment as contributing factors to developing a child's cognitive, language, and social skills. Other researchers have also challenged the stage-like growth theory, given its greater emphasis on a maturational, predetermined progression through a fixed developmental sequence – an argument for a more significant role of nature over nurture in shaping development.

Many other researchers and theorists dispute such a rigid, step-like theory of development, emphasizing a more continuous, gradual process influenced equally by brain maturation and environmental stimulation. One prominent researcher that contrasted with Piaget, Erik Erickson, and Sigmund Freud, who all supported the stage-like growth theory, is a Soviet researcher in development psychology, Lev Vygotsky. He posits a child's cognitive development as a continuous process having no terminal stage. Meaning, that development is a process beginning with birth and continuing until death. Vygotsky's theory emphasizes nurture and social contexts, such as social interactions and social learning, in guiding cognitive development. He suggests that a child's mind is influenced and formed by external factors; specifically, interactions with adults expose a child to beliefs and biases and contribute significantly to their perception of the world. This happens when parents, caregivers, and teachers/educators share their skills with children and other sociocultural factors that provide social context. Social context influencing human development includes historical peculiarities and culture (a set of accepted behaviors, beliefs, and attitudes) and language.

Language, according to Vygotsky, is a critical tool for social learning and knowledge transmission from representatives (parents, caregivers, teachers, and other adults) in the social world that are more knowledgeable about transmitting this knowledge to children and contribute to their mental development process. Vygotsky also introduced the term "zone of proximal development" (ZPD), described as the mechanism of cognitive development that includes the actual competence level of a child and the level of functions yet unavailable but in the process of maturation. Stated another way, there are two knowledge levels - the level possessed at the moment and the potential development level - and the gap is filled with the help of representatives of the social world (specifically - parents, caregivers, teachers, and other adults). This is referred to as the 'zone of proximal development.'

So, in conclusion, during the child's cognitive development process, both nature and nurture play a role in the development process. Piaget suggests that humans learn for themselves, whereas Vygotsky believed that we must assist children in their learning to learn effectively. Vygotsky's essential suggestion is that children advance when they collaborate with others who are more skilled, raising the level of independent performance, as Piaget suggests. The story of assisted performance is the zone of proximal development (Kail, 2013). Both theorists agree that learning can lead to the development process and that language plays a central role in mental development (Vygotsky's Developmental Theory: An Introduction). I wanted to present both theorists' points of view and conclusions since Piaget's stage theory was one of the first that emerged, and Vygotsky's theory, widely supported by other researchers, is considered the most relevant, as it takes the role of the social environment and social learning into account.

If shaped and nurtured flawlessly, vital elements will form the anchors and foundation for the healthy development and continuous growth of 21st-century cognitive, intrapersonal, and interpersonal skills. More on this in the next chapter when I explain the "connective tissue" that binds all three skills (cognitive, language and communication, social and emotional) and forms the foundation (embedded in the subconscious mind) for the healthy development of 21st-century skills.

We are moving on to communication and language development. We all know that babies communicate by using gestures, sounds, and expressions to share feelings and needs like hunger, sleepiness, discomfort, and joy. Vygotsky's theory of language development emphasizes social learning and the zone of proximal development.

Other theories of language development are also worth mentioning. Psychologist B.F. Skinner suggested the idea of operant conditioning. Skinner stated that children receive "rewards" for functionally using language. A typical example used to describe operant conditioning is when a child learns to say the word drink when thirsty and receives something to drink (the reward), which reinforces the use of the word drink when they are thirsty.

Jean Piaget's theory of language development suggests that children use both assimilation and accommodation to learn a language. Assimilation is making sense of new information with the information you already have in your schema (information processed and known previously).

Accommodation is changing one's schema to adapt to a new environment. According to Piaget, children first create mental structures within the mind (schemas), and from these schemas, language develops. A schema describes both the psychological and physical actions involved in understanding and knowing. If a child with a pet dog now encounters another four-legged animal like a goat and, through assimilation, utters the word "dog" via language. The child is then corrected that not all four-legged animals are dogs, and this animal is a goat, upon which accommodation occurs by adding this new piece of information to the child's existing schema in mind.

Both Piaget's and Vygotsky's theories are often compared with each other, and both have been used successfully in education. This is a critical point for understanding how to educate our youth and how each individual assimilates and accommodates knowledge leading to successful learning methods and the ability to adapt to different environments and situations. Furthermore, adaptation is a critical skill set for success in a digital world, where technology is constantly changing exponentially.

Adaptation also plays a vital role in the upskilling and reskilling of the workforce to be better equipped with 21st-century skill sets. As an educator, you should already be exposed to these concepts and understand that the processes of assimilating and accommodating knowledge are interactive. Because if a child encounters a stimulus without the capability of assimilating or accommodating it, they will fail to understand. Thus, it is essential, as educators, to understand the difference between assimilating and accommodating knowledge and acknowledge that the latter is more difficult because each student has a unique set of schemas, depending on their background and upbringing.

This leads me to the way children develop their language and communication skills via social learning and social environment per Vygotsky's theory, and the responsibilities of social representatives like parents and caregivers to play an influential role in this development. Consequently, if during the process of assimilating and accommodating via the social environment and social learning, they are filled with negative influences and language that are self-limiting and detrimental, these negative influences get stored in the schemas and form part of the belief systems in the subconscious. I have already talked about the subconscious dictating 95% of day-to-day actions, so, needless to say, the criticality of developing language and communication skills in a child's development years is to set them up for success instead of failure, especially since language and communication development play a critical role in influencing other 21st-century skills - intrapersonal skills (e.g., learning how to learn) and interpersonal skills (communication and collaboration). In later chapters, I'll shed more light on the various techniques and strategies we can use to promote communication and how to help your child build their vocabulary and language skills, which include expressive, receptive, and pragmatic language.

Last but not least – social and emotional development skills encompass both intrapersonal and interpersonal skills. They include the child's experience, expression, management of emotions, and the ability to establish positive and rewarding relationships with others (Cohen and others 2005). As you are fully aware, many social and emotional development occurs during early childhood, as they get exposed to the social environment. This development is often expressed via temper tantrums and mood swings.

As children expand their exposure to the social world, it is essential to teach them how to learn more and be conscious of their emotions and the feelings of other people. A simple strategy is for adults who are caregivers to model and reinforce appropriate behaviors that include empathy and cooperation. Healthy social and emotional development is rooted in nurturing and responsive relationships with family members and other caregivers, including those who provide care in early learning settings (i.e., social representatives). The healthy development of a child's social and emotional skills during the early childhood development stages will aid them in their capacity to experience, regulate and express a range of emotions, resulting in the development of close satisfying relationships with other children and adults and the active exploration of their environment, which leads to mental growth. We learn from interactions with objects in the world, but we especially learn within the context of relationships.

The core features of emotional development [are] the ability to identify and understand one's feelings, to accurately read and comprehend emotional states in others, to manage strong emotions and their expression constructively, to regulate one's behavior, to develop empathy for others, and to establish and maintain relationships (National Scientific Council on the Developing Child 2004, 2). As you can see, nurturing places many responsibilities on the social representatives to ensure a positive and healthy environment via their responses to different situations. In a healthy environment, the social and emotional development will unfold in predictable ways; the child will learn to develop close relationships with caregivers, soothe themselves when they are upset, share and play with others, and listen to and follow directions. However, the opposite will occur with a hostile environment and negative responses during the early childhood development stages.

It is also important to note the importance of incorporating social and emotional skills in the education system, which eventually gave rise to social and emotional learning (SEL) and creating the Collaborative for the Academic, Social, and Emotional Learning (CASEL) organization in 1994. CASEL is now considered a trusted source for high-quality, evidence-based SEL and supports educators and policy leaders in enhancing the experiences and outcomes for all PreK-12 students.

CASEL also conducted an extensive study on the lasting impact of SEL in terms of increased academic achievement and positive social interactions and decreased adverse outcomes later in life. The study was done in conjunction with Loyola University, the University of Illinois at Chicago, and British Columbia. This study compared student outcomes of those who participated in SEL and those who did not. The results showed that those who participated in SEL programs had improved classroom behavior, an increased ability to manage stress and depression, and better attitudes about themselves, others, and school. The key here was that the change in students' perceptions and increased emotional intelligence (being self and group-aware) led to long-term academic success. Many other studies show the benefits of introducing SEL programs to educational

60

institutions — benefits ranging from positive life outcomes, reduced aggression, and students learning how to cope with setbacks and even deep trauma. All of these are excellent strategies, but just like everything else that I have described, they are reactive solutions addressing problems resulting from a hostile social environment and social learning experience during the early childhood development stage.

This is one of the key reasons I was prompted to write about these resources and implore you, as responsible social representatives, to hardwire healthy skills, belief systems, and behaviors earlier. By now, I hope you see the strong parallel between early childhood development skills (cognitive, language and communication, and social and emotional) and 21st-century skills (cognitive, intrapersonal, and interpersonal), primarily of how closely intertwined these skills are in terms of forming the proper foundation and anchors, and equally important, how they can be influenced by social representatives (parents, caregivers, and educators).

In summary, I wanted to start laying the groundwork and highlight the enormous benefits of hardwiring versus rewiring the desired mindset, skill sets, behaviors, and habits via the healthy development of the cognitive, social and emotional, language, and communication skills during the early childhood development stages. It is an alternative approach that is proactive and one that lays the foundational building blocks for the healthy development of 21st-century skills and exemplary citizenship.

I leave you with this famous quote by the great Mahatma Gandhi as we conclude this chapter:

"Your beliefs become your thoughts.

Your thoughts become your words.

Your words become your actions.

Your actions become your habits.

Your habits become your values.

Your values become your destiny."

— Mahatma Gandhi

Chapter 4: The Four C's

The Increasing Dire States and the Call for Action

Currently, the world population is 7.3 billion people, and children represent approximately 2.2 billion of that number. The latest statistics from UNICEF states that 1 billion of those children (almost half) are "multidimensionally poor – without access to education, health, housing, nutrition, sanitation or water."

According to Our World in Data and SDG-Tracker (tracking UN's SDG Goals), there were a total of 263 million children that were out of school in 2014 (the latest research I could find), leading to 250 million children under five years of age being developmentally delayed. Hopefully, you can see the urgency and the dire need to help this population group, not only because they are our future but also because it is our human obligation and duty to help out those in need with simple strategies to help them be successful and more resilient in life.

My goal, besides providing visibility to and creating awareness of these dire states, is to stress the importance of the need for a healthy environment and highlight the need for an increased number of responsible social representatives that are equipped with the strategies to help nurture early childhood development skills around the globe in a healthy manner. This will provide the strong anchors that will be part of their programmed subconscious that they can tap into as a default for continuous resilience and thrive both educationally and economically.

Hence, if you are a social representative - a parent, caregiver, teacher, educator, or other adult - please make a difference by equipping yourself with the simple strategies and knowledge that are in this book to help nurture and shape healthy cognitive, language and communication, and social and emotional learning skills to our children, especially in the critical ages from birth to seven years old. Let me proceed further with these strategies, starting with what I call the four critical C's (4C's).

<u>Curiosity</u>

The first C is curiosity; Webster's dictionary defines this as "the desire to know." I would expand the definition of curiosity as 'having a strong desire (not just a desire) to learn and know something.' If you recall, at the beginning of this book, when I described my early childhood, I talked about how I was encouraged to be curious and constantly innovate. This led me to actively seek out challenges and new experiences to broaden what I had learned, further emphasizing the importance of curiosity as a key ingredient for learning.

I have already covered the need for the workforce to reskill and upskill to meet the demands required for 21st-century skills, thus the importance of lifelong learning. I will argue that curiosity is also a catalyst for innovation since it sparks the intrinsic motivation to learn, experience, and understand the environment and the world. Curiosity is another critical skill that is important to have when faced with the onslaught of the technological advancement of Industry 4.0 and an environment with increasing globalization, where we work and share our lives with so many people with different backgrounds and ages. Again, this stresses the importance of instilling the need to be curious at a young age and preparing a child to have an open mindset to allow the child to thrive in Industry 4.0.

So, now that I have mentioned mindset, I would like to take a brief moment to expand on what is a popular theme in the corporate workplace regarding mindset, specifically, the difference between having an open (allowing growth) mindset or a closed (fixed) mindset, and the various training provided to help equip the workforce on how to cultivate an open mindset. Why do corporations invest resources in this subject? Because change is the only constant, and with the current exponential technological advancement, having a growth mindset and being open to change, and being adaptive and innovative are all essential critical skills, as opposed to "nice to have" skills.

However, before I discuss the strategies used for encouraging curiosity, let's take a closer look at the mindset and what it means. It simply means a particular way of thinking or frame of mind that shapes your opinions. It is a set of mental attitudes or opinions that you have formed about a person, a thing, your capabilities, life, or the world in general, through experience, education, upbringing, culture, etc. – do you see the pattern here?

If your experience and upbringing have been positive and gained in a healthy environment, you will most likely have a positive mindset (mental attitude and set of opinions) about life, and in the same vein, you will have a negative mindset if your experiences are negative, or if you grew up in a toxic environment.

Your mindset is influenced and shaped by your experiences, education, upbringing, culture, etc., but it is also important to note that it tends to be fixed and formed quickly and, although resistant to change (especially if it is a long-held belief), it can be changed. What I am talking about here is being proactive and instilling a positive growth mindset during the early childhood development stage because it impacts not only how a child learns to perceive the world but also how they see themselves and their abilities. To summarize, the mindset has a lot to do with self-confidence, self-esteem, and self-development as a whole.

If you want to know more about mindsets, particularly about fixed and growth mindsets, I highly recommend reading Dr. Carol Dweck's book: *Mindset: The New Psychology of Success: How We Can Learn to Fulfill our Potential.* It is an indispensable resource on the two different mindsets. Here's her description of what a growth mindset means:

"In a growth mindset, people believe that their most basic abilities can be developed through dedication and hard work – brains and talents are just the starting point. This view creates a love for learning and resilience that is essential for great accomplishment. Virtually all great people have had these qualities."

Do you want your child to be great or just mediocre? I know this is a rhetorical question, but I hope you can appreciate why I went through the explanation of mindset and how you have the power as social representatives to proactively instill a growth mindset by encouraging curiosity – a strong desire to learn and know something - which is one of the key ingredients for lifelong learning.

Here are some key strategies that you, as social representatives, can use to encourage curiosity during the early child development stages to instill lifelong learning and innovativeness. I want to state it again that I strongly believe that nurturing your child's curiosity is one of the most important ways you can help him/her become a lifelong learner.

What's interesting about this is that you don't have to motivate or make your child curious or push your child to learn; you just have to nurture and provide the right environment. Research shows that children have an internal desire to learn and a motivation to seek out new experiences. There are many observable traits in a newborn that highlight how they follow sounds, faces, and objects with their eyes to form an opinion of their environment. As they get older, they often put toys in their mouth to explore the dimensions and physicality of the object and what this means for its potential as an object, and ultimately, it gives them a greater understanding of what that object serves as in the real world and what it can do, basically using all their senses to experience and explore the surrounding environment.

Here are some tips that you can use as a social representative. I have categorized them into the six different elements you need to take into account in your pursuit of nurturing a child's curiosity.

(1) Walk the Talk – Modeling

This involves creating an environment where the child learns to understand the intricacies of communication, environment, exposure and observation, resources, and independence. As a newborn, a child's mind has great potential but limited programming (some disciplines can be programmed while still in the womb, but more on this later.) Essentially, they are actively observing and soaking it all up – the good and the bad – so it falls on the social representative to create the necessary environment to ensure the lessons they are learning are productive. I'm sure you have seen how children mimic their environment; like parrots, if they hear someone say 'shit,' they will repeat it with no awareness of its significance.

A simple solution is to be an exemplary role model by exhibiting good qualities/character and deciding on the appropriate choices and actions that are essential to being a person of good character. This is because if you are compassionate, honest, trustworthy, fair, respectful, and involved in the pursuit of the greater good of your family and community, your children will see this in your everyday actions and choices. All the characteristics I have listed here are traits I observed with my mom and dad when I was a child. I also saw how their actions and behaviors gave them a sense of joy, satisfaction, and harmony and how these emotions spread to our family's collective consciousness and to the people with whom we interacted. This mindset was not taught to me, it was observed, and it is now part of my subconscious, which was programmed at a very early age. Understanding this allows social representatives to implement and cultivate these attributes at an early age to create a healthy mind that can deal with the challenges presented in the 21st century.

If you are wondering how this relates to nurturing curiosity, it showed me first-hand how one learns about themselves and others by not judging, blaming, or shaming. A good example is when my mom would feed the homeless without judging and with love. In doing this, she created an environment that would also educate me about diversity and the circumstances in which people and communities live. How you react and the actions you take when presented with these circumstances can have a huge impact. Embrace diversity and be curious about differences that help expand your mind and expose you to other circumstances, viewpoints, values, and beliefs.

(2) Seek First to Understand — Listening

Now, let's look at communication; there are several key elements here to consider. One key element would be to practice active listening and being present. How can you teach these skills? Simply by modeling behavior where you are not multitasking when you are interacting with your child. Be mindfully present and focus on your child by demonstrating active listening through your body language and interpersonal skills by either validating or repeating the question. To this day, I tell all my kids that there is a reason why God gave us two ears and one mouth, so use them the way they were designed to be used. The famous author

Stephen Covey captures this accurately in one of his best-selling books on habits by stating: "seek first to understand, then to be understood."

I cannot emphasize enough how valuable active listening and being mindfully present is to seed curiosity because communication encompasses the act of receiving, giving, and sharing information through words, tonality, and body language, whether face-to-face or online via texting, chatting, or posting (yes, words and tonality can still be expressed online through "All Caps," exclamation marks, emojis, etc.). In short, teach them to be good communicators by listening carefully (be curious and seek first to understand), speaking or writing clearly, and respecting different opinions.

Other key elements are asking open-ended questions and answering questions simply and clearly, according to your child's age and development. This simply means avoiding closed questions that only require a yes or no response/answer and practicing using questions that start with why, how, where, what, when, which, and who. These questions open up opportunities to gain further information and extend communication and interaction. Children typically have lots of questions and natural curiosity, so care should be taken that when answering their questions, it doesn't turn into an interrogation or become defensive or confrontational – this is where the tone is also important.

You also need to be comfortable with sometimes not knowing the answer and saying, "I don't know, but we can find out." This also helps with the child's ability to actively search for answers, leading to further discovery and instilling a growth mindset. Willingness to learn is a key ingredient to fresh thinking, and what better way to instill this skill than to learn, unlearn, and relearn to keep you curious and constantly innovate?

(3) Epigenetics and more

I am combining elements three through six - the elements involving the environment, exposure and observation, resources, and independence - since there is a fair amount of overlap. The first goes back to modeling; you want your child to see you pursuing interests of your own, whether it is exercising, walking in the park, gardening, or doing both indoor and outdoor activities. You also want to create an interesting environment indoors since babies are curious about their surroundings, whether it is a set of toys for variety, engaging in family activities with you and others in the family, pictures on the wall, or even rotating the toys and activities to add variety. As you expose the child to different environments and activities, it is important to also observe and follow your child's lead and encourage their natural interests because they learn so much more through activities that capture their attention.

Of course, you need to make sure that you provide an environment that is safe for the child to explore, and the key thing here is not to discourage but to redirect. A good example of redirection is to have the child take the same action in a similar but safer environment that will not cause harm to the child but still provide the opportunity for the child to use their curiosity to explore, experiment, solve problems, and learn. Provide them with a safe environment where they are independent and comfortable with uncertainty and surprises and where constant learning can take place with open-ended activities using simple materials - materials like blocks, pans, pots, etc. - that they can explore with. Do not make the mistake of telling your child what to do with the material, how to do it, or what it should look like in the end. Let your child's curiosity be his/her guide.

Finally, when it comes to resources, the digital age we live in provides us with devices, especially smart devices, that are made in a way that allows a child to intuitively navigate with ease. You can help your child develop their curiosity by using the right media and credible sources that stimulate curiosity and build their knowledge. It is important to monitor the usage and time spent using these resources and not to use or view them as an alternative to responsible parenting (you know what I mean).

So, there you have it — simple and fairly effortless bite-sized strategies you can use to instill curiosity in your child that yield numerous benefits like developing a growth mindset and interest in lifelong learning, practicing effective communication via active listening, and being present, embracing diversity, problem-solving and innovating, and leveraging reliable and credible resources responsibly.

Conscientious

The second C is Conscientiousness, and it is one of the key elements in developing the intrapersonal skills listed as one of the main critical 21st-century skills. Specifically, under the category of work ethic/conscientiousness, we include initiative, self-direction, responsibility, perseverance, grit, career orientation, ethics, integrity, and citizenship.

So, what are the key influences that lead to the healthy development of these skills during the early childhood development stages? Before we dive into this, it is important to understand that conscientiousness, according to numerous researchers, is part of the 'Big Five Personality Traits' (Power & Pluess, 2015). It is typically referred to as OCEAN (openness, conscientiousness, extraversion, agreeableness, and neuroticism) or another commonly used acronym, CANOE (conscientiousness, agreeableness, neuroticism, openness, and extraversion). Standard features associated with someone that has a high degree of conscientiousness include high levels of thoughtfulness, good impulse control, and goal-directed behaviors (B.W. Roberts et al., 2014), which echoes the 21st-century skills definition noted above as intrapersonal skills.

As I alluded to earlier, Industry 4.0 is a significant transformation, which requires a workforce that is skilled in 21st-century skills, with a strong emphasis on "soft skills." It is important to note that soft skills do not merely comprise a specific skill or ability but rather a cluster of skills and personality capabilities that describe the attitude of each of us, our compatibility with others, and how we manage social interactions, mostly in a professional environment. Additionally, there is at least a century's worth of research, including occupational research, that provides evidence that high conscientiousness is a strong predictor of consequential life outcomes, including academic performance (M. Richardson et al., 2012), marital stability, physical health and mortality (T. Bogg et al., 2004), work performance (T.A. Judge et al., 2013), and subjective well-being (P. Steel et al., 2008). This highlights the enormous importance of nurturing this skill, a skill that will pay dividends across a very broad spectrum, both personally and professionally, in the long run. Thus, it is critically important to equip social representatives with strategies to nurture this skill as part of the early childhood development stage.

Here are some easy strategies and the most effective ways of nurturing conscientiousness – modeling, highlighting the benefits of practicing, delayed gratification, and recognition of effort. The first strategy, similar to the strategy listed in nurturing curiosity, is to model the right behaviors and actions; behaviors and actions that promote the other key components of conscientiousness, namely initiative, self-direction, responsibility, perseverance, grit, career orientation, ethics, integrity, and citizenship. How would you do that? By instilling these habits and values in a child by encouraging them to want to do a certain task well and understanding the benefit of practicing something until it is understood. Also, instilling in the child the ability to delay gratification and recognize that improvement comes with work that may be repetitive and not always enjoyable, but the rewards of that work upon conclusion will be worth the effort. Of course, and equally important, you want to celebrate the results to encourage repeat performance on any task the child undertakes.

Now, your child may be too young to understand the language used to describe these methods but not too young to grasp the concept. At the very elementary level, conscientious behavior in a child starts at a very young age; they quickly learn what the right thing to do is and how to follow through with it. Some simple examples would be brushing your teeth, washing your hands after you go to the bathroom, and picking up your toys, to name a few. This behavior will only expand further as the child develops via the right nurturing and modeling of the right behavior and actions of the adult social representatives. Yes, modeling again. It is vital to provide a consistent model to learn from as the child develops and uses all their senses to absorb the environment and its influences to develop cognitively, socially, and emotionally, and in their communication and language. This also extends to showing respect to others, being responsible, cleaning up, planning, making the bed, telling the truth – you get the idea. Children, in general, love the sense of achievement that comes from exploring and learning, and as social representatives, we need to provide an environment where they can do this safely and also recognize and celebrate these small achievements with praises and words of encouragement.

You want to find ways where there isn't always a material reward (cash or toys) or punishment, but instead, provide them with the environment and opportunity to learn and explore in order to get a repeated sense of achievement that becomes an intrinsic motivation to further learn and grow. I cannot emphasize the power of exposing and modeling without any type of rewards or punishment in developing conscientiousness behaviors in a child. The important thing to stress is that learning occurs best when there is an opportunity to experiment and explore and gain a sense of achievement via each experimentation and exploration.

I do not want to downplay the difficulty in cultivating the behaviors and disciplines of responsibility, hard work, intrinsic motivation, and delayed gratification that are core to being conscientious. It requires a lot of effort from the social representatives, and they must look for the various cues and provide guidance and feedback as appropriate. The author, Malcolm Gladwell, stated in his book The Outlier: "10,000 hours of appropriately guided practice was "the magic number of greatness," regardless of a person's natural aptitude." He also said that "with enough practice, anyone could achieve a level of proficiency that would rival that of a professional. It was just a matter of putting in the time." The bottom line is that hard work has to be engaged to eventually reach the state of intrinsic motivation by giving the child enough responsibility and experience for repeated practices and delayed gratification.

One example that I came across suggests teaching a child to be conscientious through homework. Rather than nagging the child to do his/her homework, show them and model how to plan their time so that they are not rushing, instill the habit of taking pride in completing quality work that is mistake-proof and cheer them on. If they are stuck, rather than doing it for them, show them simple strategies on how to navigate challenges. The last thing you should say to a child is, "try harder." How are they going to "try harder" if they don't have any strategies to help them navigate when they are stuck?

One of the biggest challenges that I have seen, even with my friends that have kids, is showing their children the "how-to." Things like how to focus, how to plan, how to overcome stress, how to overcome failure or setbacks, and how to react to an unfavorable situation - basically adding as many tools to their tool bag so that they can reach into it whenever they face an adverse situation. It is equally important to have them share how they have used these tools and eventually improve upon these strategies (tools) or add new tools to their tool bag since they were already taught the "how-to."

One last thing I want to add here is that as social representatives, you need to practice patience and control how you react to the child's setbacks because if you react negatively, you are promoting self-suppression as opposed to self-regulation. They might think it is their fault or perceive limitations in their abilities that are caused by the reaction or negative emotions they are observing in you. This can have a lasting negative impact, not only on the child's development of his/her conscientious skills but in other areas of development as well. Let's move on to the next C.

Critical Thinking

The third C is Critical Thinking – the connective tissue (the silent C) that binds the cognitive, language and communication, and social and emotional skills, allowing them to function holistically and in tune with each other.

In my many years of professional experience, the term "critical thinking" has been loosely used and, to a degree, used as a "catch-all" phrase that is not understood by many; so much so that when I challenge others on what it means, more often than not, I get the same response — "to think critically." I'm sorry, but this is not sufficient, so I am going to break this down the best way I can to provide a detailed description of critical thinking and why I think it is the connective tissue because the quality of everything that we do is determined by the quality of our thinking. I'll also provide you with some key strategies to nurture this skill during the early childhood development stages.

To start with, the idea of critical thinking has been around since Socrates - from about 2500 years ago - who tried to understand the concept of knowledge by asking probing questions. It has constantly evolved since then through contributions from hundreds of thinkers and is more relevant than ever in the 21st century due to the need for critical thinking in life and education.

So, what is critical thinking? As stated by the Foundation of Critical Thinking, at a high level, ***"It is the intellectual discipline of "processing" information that is gathered from, or generated by various "means" as a guide to "belief and action."*** I look at it as three separate components. "Processing" (which is the first component) involves the ability to conceptualize, reason, analyze, evaluate and integrate information that is accumulated via different "means" (the second component); i.e., information that is downloaded from others, information gathered through personal experience, information that is derived from experimentation and exploration, and by other means such as reflection, reasoning, and communication.

The third component is "belief and action," and this is where the programming of the subconscious takes place, where you, as a social representative, can equip the child with the strategies to develop their critical thinking skills by nurturing the "intellectual discipline," and providing them with both the opportunity and the means to guide their beliefs and actions.

Why do I say it is the connective tissue that enhances and harmonizes all the three early development childhood skills (cognitive, language and communication, and social and emotional)? Let me explain, the cognitive skills during early childhood are where the construction of thought processes such as remembering, learning, thinking, reasoning, problem-solving, and decision-making are being developed. As explained earlier, based on Piaget and Vygotsky's research findings, this is where the operative and figurative intelligence takes place via schemas, assimilation, and accommodation. Cognitive development also involves the concept of object permanence, understanding logical relations, and cause-and-effect reasoning. More importantly, the importance of the "zone of proximal development" speaks to the range of abilities that a child can perform with assistance, but to master them would need more guidance and practice. All of these are key components of critical thinking since it shapes information and belief-generating processing skills (how information is gathered, received, and treated), and the use of these skills repeatedly to guide behavior that becomes part of the subconscious.

When it comes to language and communication skills development, it is important to note that language and critical thinking grow together and nurture each other's development. As children engage in critical thinking, their language skills expand via their use of more complex language with words like "because" and the use of phrases with "if" and "then." As their language development progresses, it aids their growing ability to think critically.

One of the key components for language and communication skills development is active listening, the ability to discern and interpret information received, and the ability to distinguish between expressive, receptive, and pragmatic language. For example, to truly understand the meaning of a book they are reading, the child needs to do more than just recognize and sound out letters and words (which in the early stages is common). As the child matures in their development stage, they also need the ability to understand the message the book is trying to convey; this is often something that is not physically written in the book but implied in the subtext, and this prompts them to seek out more information, thus enhancing the learning experience. To do this requires critical thinking skills like analyzing and problem-solving (reading between the lines), predicting, conceptualizing /abstracting, applying, etc. Encouraging a child with this kind of thinking would do wonders in preparing the child to understand the books he/she reads and how to use the information, and also instill the joy in lifelong learning and the search to know more. All these are key skills that are directly tied to the increased proficiency in the 21st-century cognitive skills of creativity and innovation, information literacy, and information and communications (ICT) literacy – use of digital technology and oral and written communication.

Finally, I would like to explain the impact and correlation between critical thinking skills and social and emotional development skills in early childhood. If you recall, I previously referenced CASEL, an organization that has a sound framework for social and emotional learning (SEL), the process where children effectively apply acquired knowledge, attitude, and skills to function effectively across many disciplines.

A key component of SEL is self-regulation ─ part of the cognitive process activity involving reasoning and making judgments based on conclusions gained from questioning, affirmation, approval, and correction. In brief, social and emotional skills refer to the ability to regulate one's thoughts, emotions, and behaviors that impact how an individual manages their emotions, perceives themselves, and engages with others. Predictably, it influences a wide range of personal and societal outcomes throughout one's life.

I truly believe that the healthy development of SEL skills is desperately needed to increase empathy and the ability to co-operate to maintain harmony, tolerance, and respect for each other and protect the common good. All of this highlights the importance of self-regulation, a key component of critical thinking that requires information processing and cognition, including the ability to act independently and reflect critically on the ever-changing and fast-paced environment.

Concerning strategies, I want to focus on things not to do because, as social representatives, we tend to default to what's in our subconscious when dealing with emotions, expressed through our words and how we react to situations. Common phrases like, "don't be afraid," "big boys don't cry," "don't be lazy," "don't be angry," "stop being sad," etc., suppress the variety of emotions such as fear, shame, anxiety, anger, etc. This plants and reinforces the belief of the child that these social and emotional feelings are bad, and eventually, they will have a negative long-term effect on their relationships with others due to their inability to deal with these emotions when they arise.

Therefore, start with choosing the right words when you see emotions like shame, fear, anxiety, or anger, and show children how to use their critical thinking skills to deal with these emotions; critical thinking skills such as identifying and recognizing emotions, identifying the root cause of the emotion, and processing emotions constructively to help guide the next steps or remedy the situation. For instance, if it is self-induced anger because the child is impatient with completing a task, not happy with the outcome, externally induced by someone else, or the environment, teach the child to set boundaries. It is okay to be angry; it is normal. But what is the appropriate behavior when this emotion shows up? The same applies to other emotions like fear, sadness, and shame. Teach the child that these are all normal emotions and not to be ignored, but rather should be understood and processed to modify our actions and behaviors that enable better decision-making, better communications, and better relationships that help us to thrive and co-exist peacefully in this social world.

Hopefully, you see the far-reaching impact of critical thinking and why I feel that this is the connective tissue that influences the high functioning of the cognitive, language and communication, and social and emotional skills, which consequently has a strong influence on developing 21st-century skills. This is especially so regarding social and emotional skills and the 'Big Five Model,' with its well-known framework in the field of social and emotional skills; skills that contribute towards openness to new experiences (open-mindedness), conscientiousness (task performance), emotional stability (emotional regulation), extraversion (engaging with others) and agreeableness (collaboration).

Compassion

The final C is Compassion. If critical thinking is the connective tissue, then compassion would be the invisible force that amplifies both the early childhood development skills and 21st-century skills to reach superior and unparalleled heights, if nurtured the right way, and makes this world a much better place. I sincerely believe that compassion is critical for early child development stages that have a far-reaching impact on adulthood.

Webster's definition of compassion is "the sympathetic consciousness of others' distress together with a desire to alleviate." **It requires sound cognitive skills to bring the awareness needed to recognize that there is suffering or unease; cognitive skills also have the ability to make you feel emotionally moved by the plight of others and not only try to understand how that might feel for you (being empathetic) but to also attempt to take action to relieve the suffering.** I get goose-bumps even just reading this sentence because I imagine how amazing this planet and society would be if this habit of being compassionate was hardwired at an early age and became part of our subconscious.

Teaching children compassion during their early childhood learning stages acts in harmony with the other 3 C's and further enhances the early childhood development skills. More importantly, incorporating compassion as part of their broader skill set will help them think creatively when faced with different situations and aid them in making decisions that inspire their life journey and their pursuit of life with purpose.

Just look at these statistics; according to the latest data from UNESCO, globally, one out of three youths experience bullying in school. In a recent joint study in the US by the National Center for Education Statistics (NCES) and the Institute of Education Sciences (IES), about 160,000 teenagers choose to skip school just to avoid being bullied. There are also many other very troubling statistics concluding that bullying is rampant, widespread, and pervasive, and it occurs in our communities, in our schools, and even in our homes, and the effects can be catastrophic.

It is also no surprise that studies have shown that one characteristic found among children who bully is a lack of empathy for victims. Also, equally important to highlight is that bullying comes in many forms, such as verbal, physical, social, and cyber-bullying, some of which are overt and others, covert. Therefore, social representatives must be aware of these forms of bullying so that they are equipped with the right strategies to curb and deal with these behaviors and be proactive in nurturing the key habits of empathy and compassion at an early age to prevent all of these ills.

So how do you cultivate this habit during a child's early development stages? One method that you have seen before and never gets old is modeling – yes, be a model for compassionate actions and words consistently. It starts as simply as showing compassion to your child and bonding with them with your words and actions. Such actions are as simple as showing kindness, patience, acceptance, and tolerance with the child and with others. As the child models your behavior, it helps them understand what others are feeling and, more importantly, the impact of their actions and the reasons behind why someone might feel or react a certain way.

All of these are great teaching moments, but it starts with modeling the right behaviors first. Remember that compassion is like a muscle; it gets stronger with practice, and you, as the social representative, have a profound influence on the development of this ability. Here are more concrete examples of how to cultivate compassion in a child's early development stages.

- **Feelings:** First, you need to be observant of and receptive to your child's reaction to every interaction you have with them and their interaction with others (you have to have your "Spidey sense" on). When you observe something (joy or discomfort), encourage them to talk about their feelings, and this will help them understand themselves as well.

- **Expression:** The key here is to help them express their emotions through language. Acknowledge and be open with your child about how they are feeling and why they feel that way. When language is still being developed, you are filling in the blanks and modeling the appropriate words.

- **Empathy:** This is the precursor to compassion and an important concept of cause and effect during every interaction. Teaching children how negativity towards others can cause negative outcomes helps them understand what the other person may feel. It will allow them to see things from another point of view and imagine how they would react in the same place.

- **Holistic:** Expanding, being compassionate holistically beyond being compassionate to fellow human beings, by encouraging care for animals and plants and to the environment in general, and by being responsible for our actions. Show them how they play an important role in helping other living things survive, thrive, and be happy, and how their actions help the sustainability of the natural resources that are available to us.

These key strategies practiced and reinforced as part of your day-to-day interaction with the child during their early development stages will have monumental positive effects.

Four C's Impact on 21st Century Skills

By now, you have a deep understanding and appreciation of how critical the 4 C's are in early childhood development stages and how simple they are to implement. Especially important is the role they play in programming the subconscious mind through habits, behaviors, and belief systems. This, in turn, directly influences the development and continuous development of 21st-century skills and builds a more conscientious society.

You also know my view on the importance of empathy and compassion being the powerful invisible forces that influence the other C's mentioned in this section.

With that lead-in, I want to conclude by highlighting an amazing organization that we should all be aware of and leverage and model what they are doing. It is called 'The Choose Love Movement,' founded by the amazing Scarlett Lewis. They are proponents of teaching children and adults around the world on how to change an angry thought into a loving one by offering free social and emotional learning programs. On their website, under the "About Us" section - https://chooselovemovement.org/about-us-2/ - there is a simple formula listed as part of the core of all their programs:

"Courage + Gratitude + Forgiveness + Compassion-in-Action = Choosing Love." At the time of writing this book, Choose Love is in all 50 states and 120 countries, serving 3 million children by using this simple yet effective formula (Courage + Gratitude + Forgiveness + Compassion-in-Action = Choosing Love).

For those of you who are not aware of Scarlett Lewis (founder), her 6-year-old son Jesse was murdered in one of the worst mass shootings in US history at Sandy Hook Elementary School in December 2012. The 'Jesse Lewis Choose Love Movement' is her plea to everyone in the world to become part of the solution to the issues that we're seeing in the world and society in general. Through her global non-profit, Scarlett is on a mission to create safer and more loving communities that offer enriching connection, resilience, and well-being to all through living a life based on the Choose Love Formula. The formula comprises the character values of Courage + Gratitude + Forgiveness + Compassion-in-Action that serves as a guide for living a Choose Love lifestyle. When practiced, they strengthen health and resilience, improve the community and culture of groups, and promote a safer, more peaceful, and loving world.

With that, I urge every single social representative across the globe to take responsibility and understand the immense power you have in nurturing our children with the right habits and behaviors during their early childhood development stages as a proactive measure to build exemplary citizens and future 21st-century leaders.

Chapter 5: Hardwiring: The Why, The What, and The How

At this point, reading Chapter 5, you now have an insight into some reasons behind the turmoil that we are seeing around the world. You are aware of the emergence and continued growth of billion-dollar industries that have sprung up to address these ills, but for the most part, they're treating the symptoms versus the root causes. We have discussed the onslaught and continuous exponential technological advancement and the need for new skills called 21st-century skills. You have also seen the close connection and the impact of the foundational skills that can be nurtured as part of early childhood development via cognitive, language and communication, and social and emotional skills to build thriving 21st-century leaders. I've also included as many empirical studies as I could to support the content provided in this book and offered examples of some of the root causes of our social, economic, and political ills. Additionally, I've included some of my personal experiences as first-hand exposure to further illustrate the power of the 4 C's.

All of this highlights the power that you have as a social representative to influence the building of future 21st-century leaders and exemplary citizens. This can be done primarily by implementing and reinforcing some key, bite-sized, simple, and practical strategies required to develop healthy childhood development skills that help shape the continuous development and maturation of 21st-century skills.

More importantly, I wanted to show you how impactful these strategies can be in shaping the subconscious, given that we operate 95% of the time with our subconscious, and last but not least, the importance of the Four C's. The Four C's can be implemented with just a little bit of effort on your end as a social representative but can have a massive, positive effect on a child in later life.

I am also hopeful that as you read this book, you, as social representatives, can also have a better appreciation and understanding of the root causes of your current limitations as you pursue your journey in rewiring or reprogramming your subconscious. It is lamentable that this resource was not available to you when you were younger and in your nurturing stages, but now that you are in the know, you have the power to not only influence others positively but also fast-track your own development and improvement processes. This summarizes "why" you need to hardwire these skills as part of a child's early development skills; now, we move on to the "what" and "how" to hardwire these skills by age group.

Ages 0 to 12 months

During this stage, when a child is between zero and 12 months old, the majority of the child's development is gained through interactions that are more likely to be initiated by a social representative. So, I want to equip you with additional resources to aid you in effectively nurturing the child's early development during this period.

First, I want to start with science. When a baby is born, the average baby's brain is about a quarter of the size of an adult's brain, and it doubles in size in the first year. It keeps growing to about 80% of adult size by age 3 and is nearly fully grown, at over 90%, by age 5. As you can see, this is tremendous growth in a short period, and a newborn baby has all the brain cells they'll have for the rest of their life. These brain cells are called neurons, and there are 86 billion neurons (the same as an adult) at the time of birth.

Neurons regulate thinking and also regulate the work of the body. In the nature vs. nurture debate, this would be the "nature" part - the raw materials that the child has to work with. But at birth, this raw material, neurons, do not have many connections to other neurons (Linden, 2019). Different areas of the brain are responsible for different abilities, and if you are not familiar with the different areas of the brain, I'll be covering these different areas to the best of my ability in a simplified manner. Many of you will be quick to point out that there are actually 100 billion nerve cells (neurons);

I agree that this was what was believed to be true for half a century - and can still be found in major texts - until neuroscientist Suzan Herculano-Houzel, an associate professor of psychological science at Vanderbilt University, devised a new way to count brain cells, and came up with a different number, which was 86 billion.

Regardless, it is a massive number of neurons. There are also many resources available that describe the different areas of the brain and how they develop. My goal is to show you the big picture first before getting into the details of your role as a social representative in this development.

At an elementary level, the connections are the strongest in the brain stem, which is responsible for survival mechanisms such as heartbeat, respiration, digestion, and the regulation of other functions essential for survival. The connections in the other parts of the brain – the occipital, parietal, temporal, frontal lobes, and limbic systems - are responsible for a variety of other capabilities such as balance, spatial understanding, hearing, language, control of emotions, concrete thinking and decision-making, all of which are still immature and waiting to be "hooked up." Therefore, a baby's job in the first three years is to build lots and lots of connections which are called synapses; each neuron can have thousands of synapses. Numerous research studies I've come across show that by the time a child reaches three years old, the child would have between 700 and 1000 synapses per second - and if you recall from earlier, each child is born with 86 billion neurons. I will let that sink in a little, so you can understand the capacity and the magnitude of the amount of information being processed.

Hint: Multiply the number of synapses per second by the billions of neurons present.

If you think that this is literally "mind-blowing," take a look at the recent Harvard University Center in Developing Child research that has now found the number of neural connections to be over 1 million new neural connections per second (Feldman, 2018), trumping the previously held scientific estimate of 700 to 1000 synapses per second. This makes it more impactful, and these 1 million connections per second are built over a long period through the various experiences we expose our child to (our "nurture").

This primarily happens through the hands-on, multi-sensory experiences via sights, sound, smell, taste, and touch, all of which are activated and are essential in building the connections that will be important in shaping their lives. Yes, they are sponges, and the experiences we expose our children to are being hardwired into their subconscious via the synapses. From the first time you expose something (positive or negative), and with the repetition of this exposure/action, you are helping build stronger connections, and those connections will eventually become permanent and effortless.

One of the key goals at this stage is to drive emotional response, which forms the synapses that eventually result in cognitive ease versus cognitive strain. Another important point to note and goes without saying, but I'll say it anyway, is that building all these connections at this age is very energy-consuming and thus, requires lots of calories via proper nutrition.

Before we proceed, let's revisit the brain stem, where the connection is the strongest at birth and is referred to as the survival mechanism. During pregnancy, you are advised to follow healthy habits and diets and reduce stress for healthy brain stem development. This is also applicable after the baby is born, as it ensures that the child feels safe both emotionally and physically because they are sensing their environment with all their senses. If a child grows up in an environment that makes him/her frightened or stressed, the brain goes into survival mode (brain stem function) and impedes the growth and development of the rest of the brain. If you recall from earlier chapters, I highlighted the negative impact of stress and how our fight-or-flight response impacts the growth systems since the energy for growth functions is redirected to enhance our survival functions.

This highlights the importance of providing a safe, caring, and responsive relationship by every single social representative that consists of an abundant amount of quality care, stimulation, and interaction during the early years of the child's development. Additionally, children from 0 to 12 months will constantly give you cues to engage by cooing, smiling, and crying, and a positive response to these cues forms positive connections in the brain and stimulates all the growth systems that are fundamental to the wiring of the brain.

In summary, a young child's daily experiences determine which brain connections develop and which will last for a lifetime. Here's what you can do as a social representative for babies between 0 and 12 months to help nurture cognitive, language and communication, and social and emotional skills.

To start with, don't shove flashcards in front of their faces. At birth, your baby can only see between eight and twelve inches from their eyes. The best way to develop a baby's brain connections from zero to 3 months is through gentle stimulation that includes talking, touching, hugging, and snuggling. The gentler and more compassionate the stimulation you give, the more secure and independent the child will be when they are older (Lally, 2006). Furthermore, a baby's cognitive abilities advance when exposed to positive sensory experiences and social interactions with adults (Lally, 2013). Sensory experiences include music since newborns possess a natural response to music.

In short, one must provide the child with an environment that is interesting to explore, safe, and filled with people who will respond to their emotional and intellectual needs. These are just some of the key nurturing principles needed for the right brain connections to develop and enhance the potential for future learning, especially since the infant's various brain parts are still immature and waiting to be "hooked up" and grow.

The Centers for Disease Control Prevention, under its "parent information section" https://www.cdc.gov/parents/index.html, has a wealth of information for parents and future parents. It includes resources on development milestones and how you, as a social representative, can help nurture the healthy development of a child's cognitive, language and communication, and social and emotional skills.

In a nutshell, at this development stage, the infant's best toy is – YOU! Infants have a definite preference for the human face, voice, touch, and smell over everything else. Therefore, you are equipped to be the infant's best toy as you speak, move, touch, and talk with them. In fact, during this stage of development, much of the babies' initial attention focuses on forming and strengthening secure connections with their caregivers (social representatives) and actively seeks this out. Marvin & Britner (2008) posit in their paper on the ontogeny of attachment (development of attachment during the first year of life) that babies at this stage are wired to react to those around them in ways that elicit interest and increase the likelihood of contact and closeness. Research has also shown that emotional wiring is the dominant activity during the first two years of brain development, as the brain builds crucial structures and pathways of emotional functioning that serve as the base for attachment, future emotional and social activity, and language and intellectual development that will follow (Schore 2000).

Now, here's the "how" on how you speak, move, touch and talk to infants, as this early stage of brain development results in how well one thinks and learns both as children and as adults. *95% of who we are consists of a set of habituation, unconscious thoughts, and unconscious emotional reactions, and from birth to age 5, a child's brain develops more than it does at any other time in life.* Here's a summary of what you could do as social representatives to encourage and nurture the healthy formation of brain connections (synapses) in our infants.

- **Unconditional love** – I've already dedicated a whole section on compassion as part of the 4 C's and want to further emphasize that love and affection are very real needs, and an infant's primary motivation does not involve control or manipulation. I'd encourage responding to an infant's request without hesitation, and this is not considered spoiling them but rather teaching them that they are important and worthy of your attention. You are teaching the infant how to communicate with others and that their needs can be met. By doing so, you are providing them with a strong sense of trust and emotional stability. In other words, you want to reduce stress (recall my earlier points on the survival mechanism/stress and its impact on brain growth). There is truly a biological need for your love that requires your tender, responsive attention and affection, allowing for the creation of strong self-esteem, safety, and comfort to enable brain growth via increased brain connections to all parts of the brain that are responsible for the other critical functions explained earlier in this book.

- **Active verbal interaction** – Critical for cognitive development. You must converse with, read to, and always engage with an infant with lots of verbal interactions. Research has shown that language stimulation at this stage results in more advanced linguistic skills than children who are not as verbally engaged by their social representatives. There is a very popular study done by Hart and Risley in 1995 that identified a remarkable difference in the early vocabulary experiences of young children. The difference was simply down to the number of words heard over a period of time. The results showed that "the average child on welfare had half as much experience per hour (616 words per hour) as the average working-class child (1,251 words per hour), and less than one-third that of the average child in a professional family (2,153 words per hour)" (Hart & Risley 2003, 8). So, here is a simple bite-sized tip: regardless of what your socio-economic status is, always practice active verbal interaction, use a wide range of vocabulary, and talk and sing with a kind voice and expression. I would even encourage self-talk and narrating your actions, as well as the things you see, feel, and experience, because your conversations, stories, and songs build the infant's vocabulary, demonstrate emotions, model ways to act, and even teach problem-solving skills. Keep in mind that the infant is constantly sensing the world with all his/her senses, analyzing everything, including you, and figuring out ways to mimic your voice and facial expressions as a way of learning about the environment and world around them.

- **The magic of touch** – Please avoid leaving an infant for long periods alone, for example, in a swing or an infant seat. I am serious about this! There is a vast amount of research proving the ill effects of neglect, with the famous one being the effect on the Romanian children that were raised in impoverished institutions during the Romanian dictator Nicolae Ceauşescu's regime. I know this is extreme, but you can look up numerous other research articles on the ill effects of neglect.

Getting off my "neglect soapbox," touch, of all the sensory experiences, is how infants know they are loved. Gently holding, cuddling, and rocking the infant provides reassurance in the face of strangeness as they make sense of the world. You will have plenty of opportunities for nurturing touches, eye contact, and interactions during

103

multiple activities with the infant, like during bathing, diapering, or feeding, and this also fosters attachment and healthy relationship building since the infant will feel safe, secure, and loved.

On the topic of touch, it is equally important to provide an environment where the infant can also experience touch at a very early age by exposing them to various surfaces, especially since touch is one of the main sensory experiences that aid in their brain growth. Give your child lots of objects to hold that are soft, rough, or slimy, and let them manipulate them. Let them explore and discover the world with their hands with activities such as pulling, pushing, picking, opening and closing, dropping, turning, etc.

- **Exposure:** Involve the infant in your routines, and let him or her experience different surroundings with the new sights, smells, sounds, and sensations that create an enriching experience. Use different modes of movement besides just the stroller, carry them in your arms or a sling, and in general, just expose them to the world with unconditional love, active verbal interaction, and lots of touches. In short, all activities and interactions increase brain connections. However, you should also be sensitive to quiet time, rest, and proper nutrition, given the enormous information processing and energy consumption that are taking place during this stage of development.

To summarize, constantly interact (play, read, communicate) and observe your child by watching and responding to their cues. They need someone special to be there when they call; they will feel loved and nurtured if you are there to respond to that call. Hold them, cradle them and hug them, as this will keep them calm, comforted, and secure. This will also aid their healthy development in the right trajectory. Start building their self-esteem by praising them often with your love and encouragement.

At this juncture, with everything that I have laid out in this book, you as the social representatives should be in a position to positively impact the healthy development of the early childhood skills that provide a strong foundation for the development of exemplary citizens that are compassionate and conscientious, with strong critical thinking skills leading to lifelong learning and the continuous development of the 21st-century skills from birth.

Now, I want to switch gears and provide you with an overview of additional strategies and upcoming resources that you can leverage for ages 1 through 5 years old. The book you are reading has been written as a prelude and a guide for an accompanying series of children's books I plan to publish. These books will be specific to age groups and focus on how to trigger the brain connections for cognitive, language and communication, and social and emotional skills development via stories. There will also be instructions available to the social representatives (again, parents, caregivers, teachers, etc.) on how to use these resources. These include practical, bite-sized exercises developed to nurture and reinforce these brain connections in a child's everyday interactions. Each age group will have three books that can be used in any order or together for the healthy development of cognitive, language and communication, and social and emotional skills. As such, below, I have included details of how to best utilize these books in a way that complements the knowledge gained here. The information is relevant, even without the accompanying children's books, so please read on.

Ages 1 Year and Beyond

As an introduction to this section detailing how the books for ages 1 through 2 years, ages 2 through 3, and ages 3 through 5 help cultivate and enrich the cognitive, language and communication, and social and emotional skills, I want to share with you a visual – Figure 1 (as seen on the page #108): The 4C's Framework for Early Childhood Development Skills. I encourage you to always keep this visual in mind as an overall framework to remind yourself of the critical role the 4 C's play in early child development stages and the key focus areas as it pertains to the development of each skill. Think of the 4 C's as the source that provides the powerful nutrients or fertilizer to nurture the healthy development of cognitive, language and communication, and social and emotional skills. Also, keep in mind the key elements within these three early childhood development skills that help form the connections in the brain.

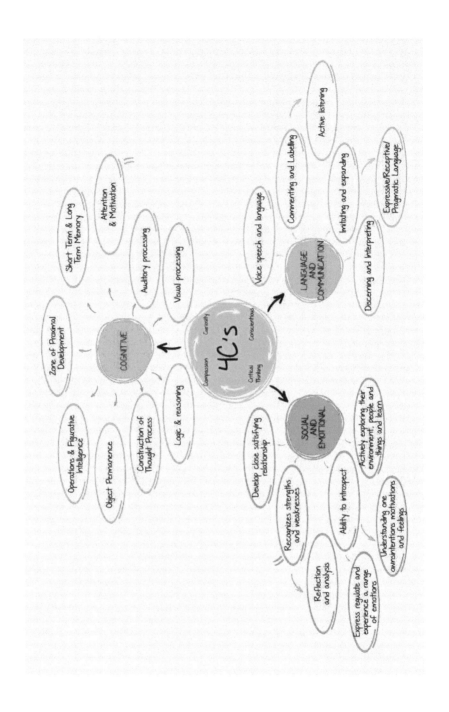

Figure 1: The 4C's Framework for Early Childhood Development Skills

In addition to the framework above, it is important to understand the sensitive period for each part of the brain development process in terms of how the different parts of the brain are growing and developing the most - remember the earlier discussion on synapses (connections) in the brain. I touched on this briefly in earlier sections of the book, but I want to take a closer look with the help of an illustration I came across by the MacMillan Cancer Support resource called the "brain map" that shows the brain skill development timeframe across the different parts of the brain. It highlights the development of thought, breathing, heart rate and temperature, balance and coordination, visual processing, language and touch, memory and behavior, hearing, learning, and emotions. It provides a detailed illustration of the sensitive period (timeframe) for the type of development skills growing and developing the most in that part of the brain. I have included the web link to the Brain Map (as seen on the page #110):

https://bellevuetoddlers.files.wordpress.com/2013/12/brain-map.pdf

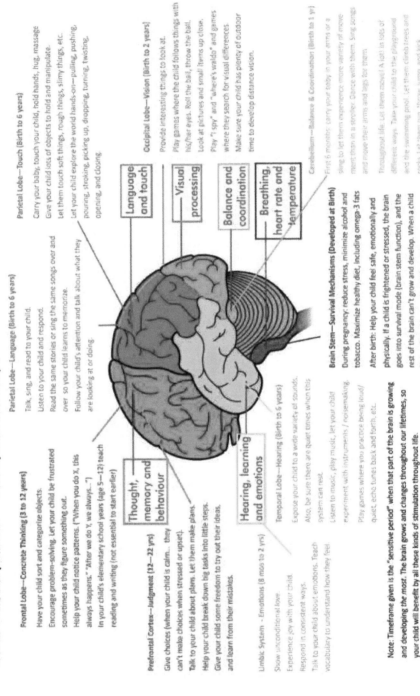

Figure 2: Brain Map

Here's a summary that is a combination of what's described by the brain map resource and the developmental milestones as described by the CDC. I would also encourage you to review and leverage both the brain map and the CDC resource:

- Brain Stem: This is developed at birth and regulates key functions essential for survival. It is the part of the brain that triggers the survival mode if it senses stress or fear and consumes all the energy towards survival, which in turn inhibits brain growth and development. As a social representative, you want to ensure that the child feels emotionally and physically safe so that the rest of the brain can grow and develop.

- Cerebellum: It is also referred to as the "little brain," which is the part of the brain that is responsible for several voluntary movements and functions such as balance, coordination, and posture (Buckner, 2013). Here's where, as a social representative, you unleash the infant's ability to explore and move in a safe environment rather than being confined in their stroller, rockers, or portable car seat during their waking hours. The sensitive period, as defined by this resource, is from birth to 1 year.

- Occipital Lobe: This is one of the four lobes within the cerebral cortex. Side note: the cerebral cortex makes up about two-thirds of the brain's total mass and lies over and around most of the brain's structures. This part of the brain –

the occipital lobe – is responsible for vision and is also referred to as the visual processing center. The sensitive period here is from birth to 2 years; thus, the importance of stimulating a child's vision during this stage, given that their depth perception is fully developed by year 1. However, as new-born, they can only see images that are a few feet away (Bushnell, 2003), and therefore, require plenty of up-close "face time" with their parents or care-giver to establish familiarity and to provide them with a sense of security.

Towards the one to 2-month phase, they can focus both eyes and track moving objects (Sheridan, 2008), and this is the stage that you as a social representative can start exposing the child to interesting and colorful pictures, images, books, toys, and even talk about the differences. As the child develops from 3 months to 12 months, continue this process and introduce different activities that are indoors and outdoors so that they can develop distance vision. Here's where the concept of object permanence emerges and kicks in. You can encourage this through simple games like peek-a-boo or partially hiding a toy under a blanket. Developing object permanence is a critical milestone, and is a precursor to symbolic understanding, which helps develop language, pretend play, and exploration and also helps children work through separation anxiety (Mazel & Murkoff, 2010). Again, refer to the CDC website for the various developmental milestones and activities you can do with the child to stimulate and develop the child's vision during this sensitive period, starting with up-close "face-time," identifying and differentiating different colors and objects, reaching and grabbing objects, pointing and progressing to telling the difference between "near" and "far."

- Parietal Lobe: This is the part of the brain that interprets the sensory world around the body by processing sensory information mainly relating to touch, taste and temperature. It is the starting point of sensory processing within the brain, whereby it receives and processes sensory information from all over the body. The sensitive period is between birth to 6 years.

I have already covered the topic of the "magic of touch" in detail, but now you know which part of the brain is being developed and the sensitive period for this development. It is also important to note that the parietal lobes also work in collaboration with other areas of the brain, influencing multiple functions beyond touch sensation (Goldberg, 2001). Here's a sampling of other parietal lobe functions: cognition, information processing, understanding spatial orientation, movement coordination, speech, visual perception, reading and writing, and mathematical computation. Therefore, as social representatives, you need to ensure that at this sensitive period, especially when it comes to the parietal lobe, development learning is filled with stimulating things and places that facilitate the child's exploration through sight, sound, smell, taste, and touch;

basically, as many sensory experiences as possible, since this forms the connections in the brain for healthy cognitive growth.

- Temporal Lobe: The temporal lobe happens to be one of my favorite lobes to talk about since it centers around auditory stimuli, memory, and emotion. Its sensitive period is from birth to 6 years. Auditory capacity is all about interpreting the various sounds and information received through the ears to give it meaning and focus on the important sounds in the environment. This includes understanding and giving meaning to language. The temporal lobe also has a visual aspect as well that helps establish object recognition (both simple and complex objects), such as faces. This is the favorite part that I alluded to earlier, where the temporal lobe is a significant part of the limbic system, which is involved with our behavioral and emotional responses. I'm sure that everyone has heard about the amygdala and hippocampus; well, these are important structures in the limbic system which are responsible for key processes in the brain, such as memory, motivation, learning, and attention. Furthermore, the temporal lobe - in interacting with these structures - plays a critical role in memory and helps to form conscious long-term memory. Why is this important? As I reiterate once again - it is critically important because *"95% of who we are consists of a set of habituation, unconscious thoughts, and unconscious emotional reactions, and from birth to age 5, a child's brain develops more than it does at any other time in life."*

The sensitive period in terms of the limbic system growing and developing the most, according to the Macmillan Cancer Support resource, is between 8 months to 2 years.

So, as a social representative, how can you provide healthy nurturing of this part of brain development? Other than what has already been covered before in the section on the 4 C's, the only other point I would like to highlight here is the importance of security and the minimizing of stress and anxiety levels of the child. This facilitates the energy distribution towards the other parts of the brain development process like the temporal lobe development. I would also encourage you to read up on the autonomic nervous system, which consists of the sympathetic (fight or flight response) and parasympathetic (rest and digest response) nervous systems and their relation to the development of the temporal lobe.

• Frontal Lobe: The Macmillan resource posits that the sensitive period for the development of the frontal lobe is between 3 and 12 years, and it is also important to note that this is the last part of the brain to fully mature with full maturation being at 25 years of age. This is also the part of the brain that is larger and more developed in humans than in any other organism. It is the "control panel" of our personality and our ability to communicate and control higher cognitive functions such as memory, emotions, impulse control, problem-solving, social interaction, and motor function. The front part of the frontal lobe is called the prefrontal cortex, and the key functions carried out by the prefrontal cortex can best be summed up as supporting the executive function, self-control, and guiding attention. These functions, referred to as judgment, as described by the Macmillan resource, have a sensitive brain development growth period being between 12 and 22 years. They give us the ability to differentiate conflicting thoughts, determine good and bad, distinguish between choices (better and best or same and different) and future consequences of current activities, work toward a defined goal, prediction of outcomes, expectations based on actions, and social control/self-regulation (Grawe, 2017).

Merely looking at these abilities, it is no surprise then that studies have shown that a well-developed prefrontal cortex with strong executive functions can improve both academic and life outcomes. I have highlighted in this book how social representatives need to model the right behavior and actions to nurture the healthy habits and development of the brain connections. Here's another reason why modeling is critical, specifically when it is related to the development of the prefrontal cortex - the presence of mirror neurons in the child's cortex gives the capacity for imitation. This gives the child a greater capacity to learn by imitating what they see and hear and even the ability to imitate another's movements and feelings. Research studies have shown that mirror neurons allow us to know what another person is feeling, without having to think about it, thus making empathy possible and leading to higher emotional intelligence and the ability to empathize with others (Carter, 2019).

Therefore, as social representatives, you need to model your executive functioning capacities to know what to say, do and think in your day-to-day life situations. The child is constantly observing every action, word, or thought that is calm, warm, kind, respectful, playful, or even acts of being creative, planning, problem-solving, or making choices. This will, in turn, fire their mirror neurons and form new connections, and develop the frontal lobes as if they were performing these actions themselves. The more positive and healthy actions, words, or thoughts repeated in front of the child, the sooner the development of the frontal lobes and the ability of the child to repeat the words and actions in a proper context. This is a very important point here regarding modeling the right actions, words, and thoughts by the social representatives because if a child does not have a chance to imitate positive models in their life, it will result in the underdevelopment of the frontal lobe. As described by Margot Sunderland in The Science of Parenting, a subsequent ill effect of this is that the child is left to be driven by ancient rage/fear and defense /attack responses deep in the mammalian and reptilian parts of the brain. Brain scans show that many violent adults are still driven, just like infants, by these primitive systems (Sunderland, 2006).

I know that I have presented some pretty heavy content as part of the brain map. I deliberately went a little deeper on the negative side effects; when there is a lack of brain connection to again show the power of proactive nurturing and wiring of the neurons to prevent most of the common ills that exist in human beings in general. With this, I'll conclude the brain development section here.

Given what we have just read, I want to return to the importance of the supplementary resources that further reinforce some of the strategies described above - the set of children's books that will be followed in the trails of this book. These books cater to ages one and beyond and have illustrations and recommended practice exercises to reinforce the right mindset, skillset, and behaviors during the early childhood development stages. I'm hopeful that these added resources will help you come up with additional innovative ways to reinforce these healthy anchors during their early childhood development stages, primarily because you now know the impact that these strategies play toward the end goal of building exemplary citizens that are critical thinkers and conscientious, with a passion for lifelong learning resulting in future 21st-century learners.

Synaptic Pruning

Another reason why reinforcement is critical is because of "synaptic pruning." If you recall from earlier, in a baby, the brain overproduces brain cells (neurons) and connections between the brain cells (synapses), and then it starts pruning back the weaker connections around the age of three, and this pruning proceeds until early adulthood. Yes, it is like the pruning of a tree and cutting the weak branches so the other branches will flourish. I often equate the brain to a garden, where you constantly need to fertilize ("the good ") for healthy growth and also pull the weeds ("the bad") out. Therefore, as a social representative, if you want a certain set of characteristics to "stick" and not have it pruned, it is important to reinforce these through reading, modeling, exploring, and experiencing.

The series of children's books, dealing with different age categories from 1 to 5 years, have many focus areas. The first set of books will focus on developing and enhancing cognitive, language, and communication skills. The second set of books for each age group will solely be focused on developing the child's social and emotional skills. Again, each book will also have practice exercises that serve as a guide for the social representatives to help leverage and extend the learning and brain development process in their interaction and the child's response and interaction as part of their daily routine (this is the reinforcement piece). One of the key elements of reading is consistency, repetition, fun, and interaction. This means it is important, first and foremost, to make sure that you make the activity of reading fun and something that the child would look forward to. Making it fun requires consistency, so try to read this book or any other book at least daily, and have the child pick their favorite book.

Research has shown that we learn best when we are happy, so making the child feel loved, cared for, and safe will allow their brain to have a high level of neuroplasticity – meaning, it will be more open, flexible, and primed for learning (Kolb, 1995).

Per my earlier comment, when we are stressed or frightened, our brain goes into survival mode and, therefore, will be less open to learning. This does not mean we don't learn when we are stressed, but that much of what we learn at the time we are stressed is how much we want to avoid having that unpleasant experience again. So, have a special reading space where there is a minimal distraction, and make sure that you involve the child in the reading activity by talking about the pictures, making sounds, amplifying certain words with rich expressions, and pointing to words. It is also equally important to teach the child to cherish and respect the book and the information that is within the book.

At an early age, reading with consistency, and involving them in the process, is all about having fun with books and modeling a love of books and reading. Also, bear in mind the sensitive periods (referring to the MacMillan's Brain Map) when the different parts of the brain are growing and developing the most by forming brain connections; synapses in areas such as language and touch, visual processing, and hearing, learning, and emotions. All of these contribute to the child's cognitive development since cognitive development refers to how a child perceives, thinks, and gains an understanding of their world through the interaction of genetic and learned factors that include information processing, intelligence, reasoning, language development, and memory. Essentially, it involves nurturing via all the key elements described above in **Figure 1: The 4C's Framework for Early Childhood Development Skills,** and taking advantage of this resource to improve cognitive skills through practicing patterns and sequencing, math concepts such as counting and observation of differences, ability to practice recall and connecting from repetition and previous knowledge – memory.

Regarding speech and language, the first three years of a child's life is the most intensive period for acquiring speech and language skills, as further emphasized by the research study by Hart and Risley (1995, 2003) that I've cited in earlier chapters. These skills develop best when a child is exposed to a world that is rich with sounds, sights, and consistent exposure to the speech and language of others. I can personally attest to this since I spoke three different

121

languages by the age of 5, and I'm still able to speak these languages. All of these started with the rich and consistent exposure to the speech and language of others.

Regarding sounds, music has amazing effects on the child's development that goes beyond words. It improves spatial-temporal reasoning, and for that reason, there will be multiple opportunities to sing along in the accompanying children's books, along with some simple strategies to improve spatial intelligence via songs and musical instruments. Side note – since it is a critical development area – spatial refers to space, and temporal refers to time; hence, spatial-temporal reasoning is how the mind processes its knowledge of space and time. Described in a different way, it is the ability to see a disassembled picture and mentally piece it back together. More so, the analysis and visualization through spatial-temporal can be challenging. Thus, it is important to introduce key techniques during this stage of child development to improve spatial-temporal reasoning since it is key for problem-solving and organizational skills.

Another key area that the children's books will focus on is the development of the child's phonological awareness. Phonological awareness (connected to the development of the occipital and temporal lobe) is a strong predictor of success in learning to read and spell. Phonological awareness, in simple terms, means the awareness of sounds in spoken words, as well as the ability to manipulate these sounds. This is a key skill for decoding printed words, and it is a purely auditory and oral skill. Phonemic awareness is the awareness of and ability to manipulate the individual sounds (phonemes) in spoken words (Kilpatrick, 2015). It is a critical skill for the development of both spoken and written language.

Essentially, there are five levels of phonological awareness: rhyming, alliteration, sentence segmenting, syllable blending and segmenting. Rhyming involves rhymes, rhythm, and repetition, intending to help with the recognition of rhymes and the production of rhymes. For example, the ability to recognize common sounds in words like the /og/ sound in "dog" and "log" or the /at/ sound in "cat" and "bat." If you ask a child to respond to a similar word to "wow," and the child responds with "cow," it would be an example of the ability to produce rhyming words when asked. Alliteration is wordplay when words share the same initial sounds and develops the child's ability to recognize the words that have the same beginning sound – examples would be apple, ants, alligator, etc.

The key to sentence segmenting and syllable blending is to understand that sentences can be segmented into words, and words can be segmented into syllables. This helps the child understand that sentences are composed of separate words in a particular order to convey meaning. The key here is to start with the words, understand how many syllables are in each word (segmenting), and put those syllables back together (blending), for example: "win-dow" or "won-der-ful" (segmenting) and "window" or "wonderful" (blending). Then you move to sentence segmentation – "this is a glass window" – and have the child identify how many words there are in the sentence.

To summarize, there will be various categories of phonological development skills incorporated in the books that will include word segmentation, recognition of rhymes, production of rhymes, mastery of syllables (including syllable recognition, deletion, substitution), and sound skills starting with sound/phoneme recognition that includes sound imitation, isolation, blending, substitution and segmentation. I'll stop here before I start including snippets of the entire book series. Rest assured that I will highlight the key development areas and brain connections that are being targeted in the practice sections in each book for the healthy development of the cognitive, language, and communication skills during a child's early development stages.

The second book on developing social and emotional learning focuses on the child's experience, expression, and management of emotions. It teaches the child how to establish positive relationships with others. I can't emphasize enough the importance of the 4C's for this skill development, and therefore, some of the key messages in this book would include examples of modeling good behavior, listening and following directions, empathy, and the joy of being empathetic, encouraging cooperation, and the benefits and harmony that accompany these behaviors.

It is also important to highlight that one of the critical parts of the brain in developing social and emotional skills is the prefrontal cortex. I touched on this earlier, but here's a more in-depth analysis of the prefrontal cortex, which has 9 major functions that form an individual's emotional well-being. It is responsible for bodily regulation, attuned communication with others, emotional balance, response flexibility, fear modulation, empathy, insight, moral awareness, and intuition (Siegel, 2007). Dr. Siegel posits that all these 9 functions support mental, physical, and relational health, and if found to be imbalanced, it can be supported by mindful awareness practices like meditation and other mindfulness cognitive therapy. What is amazing, however, is the fact that the majority of these 9 functions are easily influenced in the early childhood development stage via nurturing by a parent and various social representatives. Here are a few examples – attuned communication and empathy are the ability to feel the other person's feelings, and, as I touched on earlier, a child needs to be attuned in order to feel secure for healthy development. Other functions such as response flexibility – the ability to pause before action – and evaluating the morality and consequences of subsequent actions (thinking beyond self and the larger social good) all come from modeling these behaviors as a social representative. The key emphasis here is nurturing and modeling the right behaviors to develop the 9 functions of the prefrontal cortex that support mental, physical, and relational well-being during the early childhood development stages.

The end goal here is two-fold; first, to provide the right anchors for cultivating healthy social and emotional skills, and secondly, to provide the techniques or discipline needed to realign ourselves with our core. What do I mean by "realigning ourselves with our core"? There might be occasions when an individual might slip and say or do something that they know is "not right" (e.g., being insensitive or doing something that is not favorable) due to any number of internal or external factors such as peer pressure. However, the hope is that because of the subconscious programming of our brain that is embedded with healthy social and emotional skills, it is only a "momentary slip," and we can realign to our normal empathetic self and say and take the right actions.

I want to conclude this book by inviting you to further your knowledge of the subject by using the collection of children's books and appealing to all like-minded individuals, like Scarlett Lewis of the ChooseLoveMovement.org and others, to join forces and be inspired to leverage whatever resources or expertise you have at your disposal, in order to provide and promote a positive influence to our children and adults across the globe.

EPILOGUE

My journey started with my quest to discover what the root cause for all the upheavals in the world is, specifically the social, economic, and political ills. After researching multiple resources, including evidence from numerous research studies, I found a common theme – **our habits and belief systems.** This, in turn, led me to explore how each human being's actions and inactions are formed and motivated, resulting in the discovery that 95% of brain activities are unconscious. More specifically, *95% of who we are consists of a set of habituation, unconscious thoughts, and unconscious emotional reactions.*

Gretchen Rubin masterfully labeled our habits as the "invisible architects of our life." This is an important baseline for understanding that led me to write this book and use this premise to connect the dots between brain development during early childhood development skills (including the critical development period), the influences of each individual's genes, the role of the social representatives, and the environment (epigenetics) that shapes our habits and belief systems.

Once this connection was unlocked and corroborated by multiple research studies, this book further showed, with support of research evidence, the impact on the healthy or unhealthy development of the early childhood development skills in adulthood – both the positives and negatives. It also highlights the direct correlation and importance of nurturing and the environment (epigenetics) to the development of these early childhood development skills.

I further showed how the majority of the solutions that currently exist to "cure" our ills are more reactive and tend to treat the symptoms rather than the root cause. There are multi-million and billion-dollar industries that have sprung up to help "fix" the habits and belief systems that are causing these ills. I want to make it very clear that I am not knocking these industries with their multiple resources, primarily because these habits have been deeply embedded and, therefore, require outside assistance to rewire these habits.

This is one of the reasons I highlighted how you can use the knowledge gained in this book, how individual habits and belief systems were formed in the first place, and how to identify them in order to accelerate your healing. This is why chapter 4 is titled "a proactive and complementary solution."

More importantly, I'm speaking directly to the social representatives in a bid to educate and provide them with the resources to proactively shape and nurture the healthy development of habits and belief systems. I also provided my example as a child that grew up with modest means yet, in an environment that was abundant with the 4 C's. In addition, I included my first-hand experience in my professional life over three decades and, most importantly, the various substantiated research studies.

I also strongly believe that I barely scratched the surface on the impact of the 4 C's and, in addition to this book, if you were to do your research, you would find numerous research studies that support the power of nurturing, as well as the impact of the 4 C's in early childhood development and its impact on social, mental and health wellness in adulthood. To me, the 4 C's are common sense, but too often, we are caught up in our emotional states as parents, owing to our upbringing, and as a result, face multiple societal pressures - both warranted and unwarranted - and tend to just make a "good enough" effort on the 4 C's as opposed to going full-out during parenthood. I am saying this not because I want you to feel guilty or be ashamed of yourself, especially if you have already made mistakes with your other children, but more so to acknowledge this fact. It is never too late to course-correct. Pause, slow down, and keep in mind what is important in life, especially since the children are our future, and we are in this rat race because we want to give them a better life.

Simple and practical strategies to instill the habits of curiosity, conscientiousness, critical thinking, and compassion will also be embedded throughout the children's book via the stories, examples, and simple exercises so that they can be reinforced repeatedly with the end goal of storing (hard-wiring) these skills in the child's subconscious mind. The beauty is, by practicing 4 C's, along with you being an excellent role model, it does not cost a penny, and you do not need expensive toys and gadgets to help them develop their cognitive, language and communication, and social and emotional skills.

I also articulated the strong parallels between the early childhood development skills, consisting of cognitive, language and communication, and social and emotional skills, and the 21st-century skills, namely the cognitive, interpersonal, and intrapersonal skills. More specifically, it is pertinent to instill the habit of lifelong learning - an essential skill in the development of 21st-century skills - especially when the need relates to the need to reskill and upskill.

In the end, it all starts with the 4 C's, where critical thinking skills are the connective tissue, and compassion is the invisible force to help form the anchor for the development of early childhood development skills and the continuous development of 21st-century skills.

Also included is a reference to the critical social and emotional skills and the realization and focus by many organized bodies on social and emotional learning, which in my opinion, is the foundation for building exemplary citizenship.

I also focused on equipping you with all the knowledge and resources, such as the 4 C's framework and the connection to the various skills' development, details on the brain map and the development of the different parts of the brain via synapses, and the associated skills and their critical periods. These highlight the development of the different parts in the temporal lobe that are directly influenced by proper nurturing.

So, with this book alone, you as a social representative will be well-equipped to play an instrumental role in the healthy development of early childhood development skills.

Therefore, the children's books for ages 1 through 5 years, which focus on cognitive and language and communication skills, and social and emotional skills, are primarily a complementary and critical resource for reinforcing these nurturing techniques; view it as an operating manual for a social representative, and a resource for the social representative to reinforce the learning as a means to enhance and harden the development of the child's brain synapses so that they do not fall victim to the pruning effect. It is a companion guide that takes everything that I have mentioned in this book in a form that is fun, interactive, and effectively presented in bite-sized stories that nurture and enhance the development of early childhood skills.

Before I conclude, I want to stress the importance of the influence of the environment - epigenetics - which I am constantly fascinated by. It was one of the major influences in writing this book. I also wanted to briefly describe and highlight the vast resources and emphasis placed on the "habits of the mind" since there are key elements of this discipline incorporated in the upcoming children's books.

Epigenetics is the field of study that looks at how environmental influences, such as diet, physical activity, stress, and even environmental toxic exposure, can cause genes to activate or turn off while not changing the DNA sequence itself. For a brief explanation of DNA - and if you are interested in knowing more and want to geek out on DNA and DNA sequencing - you can look up the National Human Genome Research Institute.

In brief, however, Deoxyribonucleic acid (DNA) is the hereditary material in humans that contains all of the information necessary to build and maintain an organism. All living things have DNA within their cells, and every cell in a person's body has the same DNA (this is the "nature" part of the frequently debated nature versus nurture argument). So, in summary, your genes play an important role in your health (physical and mental), and unlike genetic changes, epigenetic changes are reversible and do not change your DNA sequence, *but they can change how your body reads a DNA sequence.* This is called gene expression, which is the process by which instructions in our DNA are converted into a functional product, such as a protein (Cole,

2009); this is a simplified explanation since there is more to it in terms of transcription and translation of the DNA. Essentially, this is the on/off switch I spoke about earlier that controls when proteins are made and also acts as a volume control that increases or decreases the number of proteins made. Why is this important? Because proteins are the building blocks of life, they form the basis of our living tissues and play many different roles in our body, including a central role in our biological processes.

Hopefully, you can now appreciate why epigenetics currently stands at the center of modern medicine because it constantly changes, unlike DNA sequence, which is the same in every cell. I also hope that you have the same excitement and enthusiasm that I have in knowing how we, as social representatives, through epigenetics (nurturing via the 4 C's) and instilling good behaviors and belief systems during the child's early development stages, will make a monumental difference throughout a person's life.

More importantly, epigenetic changes occur before you are born, thus the importance of a pregnant woman's environment and behavior during pregnancy since it can change the baby's epigenetics (Roseboom, 2019). As I pointed out earlier, your epigenetics change throughout your life and your epigenetics at birth are not the same as your epigenetics during childhood or adulthood. Stated differently to further emphasize this point, your environment, your experience, and your thoughts play a major role in controlling your biology by influencing your gene expression. This means that genes are not "set in stone," and it is not nature versus nurture, but both, because the genes children inherit from their parents provide information that guides their development.

However, the experiences during development rearrange the epigenetic marks that govern gene expression. The collection of these epigenetic chemical marks is known as the epigenome (Dobbs, 2013). This further emphasizes that the epigenome can be affected by positive experiences that include supporting, loving relationships and opportunities for learning or negative life experiences of stressful life circumstances and negative influences like environmental toxins. Furthermore, these chemical marks or epigenetics "signatures" on genes can be temporary or permanent, and this fact further motivated me to write the book on the need to hardwire the epigenome (proactively in early childhood) versus rewiring the epigenome (reactively in later stages of life). This is important because a child is born with 86 billion neurons and would have trillions of synapses (brain connections) by the time he/she reaches three years old. Therefore, it is a gift, a blessing, and an immense responsibility for you as social representatives to provide supportive, nurturing, and rich learning experiences to the early childhood brain development stages, especially the prefrontal cortex development - the brain region responsible for judgment, planning, decision-making, and overall executive control. I might be an optimist, but if every social representative has this knowledge and is disciplined enough to practice and reinforce this teaching and modeling, it is "game, set and match"/ "game over."

Regarding the term "habits of mind," it was penned first by Horace Mann, a U.S. educator (1796-1859). He observed that "habit is a cable; we weave a thread of it each day, and at last, cannot break it." Hopefully, this resonates with my strong desire and drive to write this book in hardwiring the right habits during the early childhood development stages so that it is woven in.

Over time, Dr. Bena Kallick and Dr. Arthur Costa (2000) came up with the "16 Habits of Mind" as a result of their ground-breaking and decades-long research on how humans successfully face challenges. These 16 common habits of mind, as defined by Art Costa and Bena Kallick, serve as a set of mental skills a student can use to troubleshoot and problem-solve the situations and moral dilemmas to which the answers are not immediately known. Let me repeat – "mental skills within an individual" that are hardwired and can be retrieved to excel in any situation and function effectively in society. These 16 habits of mind are: persistence; keeping impulsivity in check; listening with understanding and empathy; thinking flexibly; thinking about thinking; striving for accuracy; questioning and posing problems; applying past knowledge to new circumstances; thinking and communicating with clarity and precision; gathering data through all senses; creating, imagining and innovating; responding with wonderment and awe; taking responsible risks; finding humor ; thinking interdependently, and remaining open to continuous learning (Costa & Kallick, 2000).

If you do a quick internet search on "habits of mind," you will see many different bodies, including educational bodies and educators, adopting these 16 habits or variations of them to improve our current methods of teaching and to better prepare our youth for our ever-changing world. It is a welcomed alternative approach to what is mostly practiced now, in preparing our youth with a focus on curriculum, rote memorization, and administering test problems with known answers.

The growing popularity of the focus on the habits of mind for educating our youth is just another piece of evidence that suggests how the early nurturing process by parents and social representatives will have a lasting effect on the kind of person that a child grows up to be. I've tried my best to illustrate the evidence of this effect with research and also covered a broader perspective that shows the interconnectedness and the importance of hardwiring the right mindset, skill sets, and behaviors during early childhood in building exemplary citizenship and future 21st-century leaders.

I hope that every parent can read my book and be able to use all the simple and practical guides available in this book and the children's books to come so that we can all do our part in shaping a loving, peaceful, and conscientious society for many years to come.

ACTION PLANNING

Before I close with my acknowledgments, I want to challenge every social representative (parents, caregivers, and educators) that is reading this book to take the following actions. I am a firm believer that unless you take notes and write down the list of actions you want to take as a result of this new knowledge, nothing will ever materialize. So, my question to you is, what are you going to do differently now that you have this new knowledge? What actions are you going to take? If you are stuck, here are some pointers using the "START, STOP, CONTINUE" method.

➢ Jot down the list of things that you are already doing well and make sure that you **continue** with these actions.

➢ Identify all your current habits and actions that are not aligned or perhaps detrimental to the healthy development of early childhood skills. Once you have done this, **stop** immediately with these habits and actions – "cease and desist."

➢ Next, list all the corrective actions that you need to **start** implementing to gain alignment. Leverage the 4 C's Framework (Figure 1) and the Brain Map (Figure 2) on the brain development period to serve as a guide to your corrective actions.

➢ Look for clusters of actions that you can incorporate as part of your routine in your daily interaction, nurturing, and education of the child.

➢ Leverage the CDC website that was referenced in this book to monitor development milestones

➢ Finally, I want to hear from each one of you – your successes, your challenges, your questions. I encourage you all to reach out if you have any questions and to also share any new ideas, techniques, or "hacks" that you stumbled upon that would help other social representatives.

I have included a detailed list of references and citations that I used for this book. I hope that you can navigate through these references if there is an area that you want to get a deeper understanding of. I am also fully aware that scientific literature changes over time; I found this even during my journey in writing this book, and so the references for this book may need to be updated. With that said, if you feel that any of the references are incorrect or if I have not referenced a source or not given credit to someone where it is due, please email me at info@drrajaratnam.com so that I can fix it promptly.

It has been a pleasure sharing my work with you. I encourage you to visit my website at www.drravirajaratnam.com, which has many of the key resources that I have used in writing this book. The website is where I'll add additional key insights on early childhood development along with any latest scientific research on this topic.

Website: www.drravirajaratnam.com

Email: info@drrajaratnam.com

Instagram: dr_ravirajaratnam

Twitter: @Ravi_Rajaratnam

ACKNOWLEDGMENTS

This, by far, is the most difficult part of the book because I have many people to thank, either directly or indirectly, that has provided me with the knowledge, discipline, time, patience, and fortitude to complete this book.

First, I have to thank all the instrumental women in my life, starting with my mom. My late, loving mom, a woman who was just 5 feet tall, and although she never worked professionally and was a homemaker, was one of the most intelligent, resourceful, compassionate, and resilient women that shaped the majority of who I am today.

A close second is my oldest sister, who basically "whipped" me into shape and taught me how to excel in everything that I did. She taught me to be fearless and relentless.

Additionally, my two most precious women who supported me in their journey; first, my wife, who gave me space, sacrificed our time together, and encouraged me, allowing me to spend endless hours writing this book. She is my rock and an incredible mother to our children. I've learned a lot from her by watching her care for and nurture our children, full of compassion and unconditional love. Thank you, my love; this book would not be possible without your selfless sacrifice and support.

Next - is my daughter, who would probably be surprised by the acknowledgment. Honey, you are my light. It is an ultimate joy to be your father, and you might not be aware, but there are a lot of things that I learn from you through our interactions, especially during our long walks together.

I'd also be remiss if I didn't thank all the amazing women leading numerous organizations across the globe in a nurturing way, a way that is a great example for others to follow.

I also want to acknowledge my two sons, who had to constantly listen to my excitement as I progressed through my journey in writing this book. Also, I can't forget the rest of my siblings and family members; each one of you is a part of my life and learning.

And last but not least, all the mentors, thought leaders, and subject-matter experts, alive and dead, have been influential in my love for learning. All these resources and support gave me the courage to write this book, and it would be a blessing if I could influence even a handful of individuals, both adults, and children, positively and pay it forward to others in making a difference in this world.

I leave you with this one quote that I came across and do not know the source, but there are many variations of this quote, and this is the one that I liked:

"If an egg is broken from an outside force, life ends. If an egg is broken from the inside, life begins. Great things always begin from inside."

You now have the power as social representatives to forever shape the insides of every child via proper nurturing of their skill development that shapes their habits and belief systems.

REFERENCES

Buckner, R. L. (2013). The cerebellum and cognitive function: 25 years of insight from anatomy and neuroimaging. Neuron 80, 807-815. doi:10.1016/j.neuron.2013.10.044

CrossRefPubMedWeb of ScienceGoogle Scholar

Bushnell IWR. 2003. Newborn face recognition. In Pascalis O, Slater A eds. Face processing in infancy and early childhood: current perspectives. New York: Nova Science. 41-54

B. W. Roberts, C. Lejuez, R. F. Krueger, J. M. Richards, P. L. Hill, What is conscientiousness and how can it be assessed? Dev. Psychol. 50, 1315–1330 (2014). CrossRefPubMedGoogle Scholar

Carter, R. (2019). The Brain Book: An Illustrated Guide to Its Structure, Functions, and Disorders. United Kingdom: Dorling Kindersley Limited.

CASEL. (n.d.). Retrieved April 17, 2021, from https://casel.org/

Centers for Disease Control and Prevention. (n.d.). Retrieved April 17, 2021, from https://www.cdc.gov/

Cohen, J., and others. 2005. Helping Young Children Succeed: Strategies to Promote Early Childhood Social and Emotional Development. Washington, DC: National Conference of State Legislatures and Zero to Three. (accessed on December 7, 2006)

Cohen S, Janicki-Deverts D, Doyle WJ, et al. Chronic stress, glucocorticoid receptor resistance, inflammation, and disease risk. Proc Natl Acad Sci U S A. 2012;109(16):5995-5999. doi:10.1073/pnas.1118355109

Cole, S. W., M. E. Kemeny, et al. (1996). "Accelerated course of human immunodeficiency virus infection in gay men who conceal their homosexual identity." Psychosomatic Medicine 58(3): 219-231.

Cole, Steve (2009). "Social Regulation of Human Gene Expression." Sage Current Directions in Psychological Science 18(3): 132-137.

Costa, A., & Kallick, B. (2000). Habits of Mind: A developmental series (Book I: Discovering and Exploring Habits of Mind; Book II: Activating and engaging Habits of Mind; Book III: Assessing and reporting on Habits of Mind; Book IV: Integrating and sustaining Habits of Mind). Alexandria, VA: ASCD.

Dobbs, D. (2013, September 03). The social life of genes: Shaping your molecular composition. Retrieved April 17, 2021, from https://psmag.com/social-justice/the-social-life-of-genes-64616

Feldman, |. (2018, September 27). New research shows significantly more neural connections formed during early years than previously thought. Retrieved April 17, 2021, from https://www.ffyf.org/new-research-shows-significantly-neural-connections-formed-early-years-previously-thought/

Frey, C. B., & Osborne, M. (2013, September 17). The future of employment: How susceptible are jobs to ... Retrieved April 17, 2021, from https://www.oxfordmartin.ox.ac.uk/downloads/academic/The_Future_of_Employment.pdf

From Neurons to Neighborhoods : The Science of Early Childhood Development. (n.d.). Retrieved April 17, 2021, from https://www.zerotothree.org/early-development

García, Emma, and Elaine Weiss. 2017. Key Findings from the Report "Education Inequalities at the School Starting Gate." Economic Policy Institute

Grawe, K. (2017). Neuropsychotherapy: How the Neurosciences Inform Effective Psychotherapy. United Kingdom: Taylor & Francis.

Hart, B., & T.R. Risley. 1995. Meaningful Differences in the Everyday Experience of Young American Children. Baltimore: Brookes.

Hart, B., & T.R. Risley. 2003. "The Early Catastrophe: The 30 Million Word Gap by Age 3." American Educator 27 (1): 4–9. www.aft.org/pdfs/americaneducator/spring2003/TheEarlyCatastrophe.pdf.

How Early Experiences Affect Brain Development. (n.d.). Retrieved April 17, 2021, from https://www.zerotothree.org/early-development

John Hopkins Medical Institutions. "Our genome changes over lifetime, and may explain many 'late-onset' diseases". (2008, June 25). Retrieved April 17, 2021, from https://www.sciencedaily.com/releases/2008/06/080624174849.htm

Khandaker GM, Zuber V, Rees JMB, et al. Shared mechanisms between coronary heart disease and depression: findings from a large UK general population-based cohort. Mol Psychiatry. Published online March 19, 2019. doi:10.1038/s41380-019-0395-3

Kilpatrick, D. A. (2015). Essentials of assessing, preventing, and overcoming reading difficulties. Hoboken: John Wiley & Sons.

Kolb, B. (1995). Brain plasticity and behavior . United States: Lawrence Erlbaum Associates.

Lally, J.R. 2006. "Metatheories of Childrearing." Chap. 2 in Concepts for Care: 20 Essays on Infant/Toddler Development and Learning, eds. J.R. Lally, P.L. Mangione, & D. Greenwald, 7–14. San Francisco: WestEd.

Lally, J.R. 2013. For Our Babies: Ending the Invisible Neglect of America's Infants. New York: Teachers College Press.

Linden, D. (2019, November 26). Think tank: Forty neuroscientists explore the biological roots of human experience: Paperback. Retrieved April 17, 2021, from https://www.barnesandnoble.com/w/think-tank-david-j-linden/1127138124

Liu YZ, Wang YX, Jiang CL. Inflammation: the common pathway of stress-related diseases. Front Hum Neurosci. 2017;11:316. doi:10.3389/fnhum.2017.00316

M. Richardson, C. Abraham, R. Bond, Psychological correlates of university students' academic performance: A systematic review and meta-analysis. Psychol. Bull. 138, 353–387 (2012). CrossRefPubMedGoogle Scholar

Manyika, J., Lund, S., Chui, M., Bughin, J., Woetzel, J., Batra, P., . . . Sanghvi, S. (2019, May 11). Jobs lost, jobs gained: What the future of work will mean for jobs, skills, and wages. Retrieved April 17, 2021, from https://www.mckinsey.com/featured-insights/future-of-work/jobs-lost-jobs-gained-what-the-future-of-work-will-mean-for-jobs-skills-and-wages

Marvin, R.S., & P.A. Britner. 2008. "Normative Development: The Ontogeny of Attachment." Chap. 12 in Handbook of Attachment: Theory, Research, and Clinical Applications, eds. J. Cassidy & P.R. Shaver, 2nd ed. New York: Guilford.

Mazel, S., Murkoff, H. (2010). What To Expect The 1st Year [rev Edition]. United Kingdom: Simon & Schuster UK.

Mokdad AH, et.al. Actual Causes of Death in the United States, 2000. JAMA. 2004; 291:1238-1245.

National Scientific Council on the Developing Child. Winter, 2004. "Children's Emotional Development is Built into the Architecture of Their Brains" Working Paper No. 2. (accessed on December 5, 2006)

National Academies of Science, National Research Council (2012). Education for Life and Work: Developing Transferable Knowledge and Skills in the 21st Century. National Academies Press. doi:10.17226/13398. ISBN 978-0-309-25649-0.

Neugebauer, B., ed. 1992. Alike and different: Exploring our humanity with young children. Washington, DC: NAEYC.

P. Steel, J. Schmidt, J. Shultz, Refining the relationship between personality and subjective well-being. Psychol. Bull. 134, 138–161 (2008). CrossRefPubMedGoogle Scholar

Power RA, Pluess M. Heritability estimates of the Big Five personality traits based on common genetic variants. Transl Psychiatry. 2015;5:e604.

ReportLinker. (2020, December 29). Global soft skills training industry. Retrieved April 17, 2021, from https://www.globenewswire.com/news-release/2020/12/29/2151198/0/en/Global-Soft-Skills-Training-Industry.html

Roseboom T., Epidemiological evidence for the developmental origins of health and disease: effects of prenatal undernutrition in humans external icon. J Endocrinol 2019. 242:T135-T144

Sel: What are the core competence areas and where are they promoted? (n.d.). Retrieved April 17, 2021, from https://casel.org/sel-framework/

Schore, A.N. 2000. "Attachment and the Regulation of the Right Brain." Attachment and Human Development 2 (1): 23–47.

Sheridan M. 2008. From birth to five years: children's developmental progress. London: Routledge

Siegel, Daniel J. The Mindful Brain: Reflection and Attunement in the Cultivation of Well-Being. New York: W.W. Norton, 2007.

Starting Smart: How Early Experiences Affect Brain Development. (n.d.). Retrieved April 17, 2021, from https://www.zerotothree.org/early-development

Sunderland, M. (2006). Science of Parenting: Practical Guidance on Sleep, Crying, Play, and Building Emotional Well-being for Life. United Kingdom: DK.

Szegedy-Maszak, Marianne (2005). "Mysteries of the Mind: Your unconscious is making your everyday decisions." U.S. News & World Report.

T. Bogg, B. W. Roberts, Conscientiousness and health-related behaviors : A meta-analysis of the leading behavioral contributors to mortality. Psychol. Bull. 130, 887–919 (2004). CrossRefPubMedGoogle Scholar

T. A. Judge, J. B. Rodell, R. L. Klinger, L. S. Simon, E. R. Crawford, Hierarchical representations of the five-factor model of personality in predicting job performance: Integrating three organizing frameworks with two theoretical perspectives. J. Appl. Psychol. 98, 875–925 (2013). CrossRefPubMedGoogle Scholar